The Riot and the Dance
Teacher's Guide

THE RIOT AND THE DANCE

TEACHER'S GUIDE

OBJECTIVES
QUIZZES & EXAMS
ANSWER KEYS

DR. GORDON WILSON

ILLUSTRATED FORREST DICKISON

canonpress
Moscow, Idaho

Gordon Wilson, *The Riot and the Dance: Teacher's Guide*
Copyright © 2018 by Gordon Wilson, PhD.
Illustrations copyright © 2018 by Forrest Dickison.

Published by Canon Press
P.O. Box 8729, Moscow, Idaho 83843
800.488.2034 | www.canonpress.com

Cover design by James Engerbretsen. Cover illustrations by Forrest Dickison.
Interior design by Laura Storm Design. Interior Layout by Valerie Anne Bost
Printed in the United States of America.

18 19 20 21 22 23 24   10 9 8 7 6 5 4 3 2

CONTENTS

PART 1: THE LIVING CELL

UNIT 1

{1} A Smidge of Chemistry.................................3

Chapter 1 Quiz.................................5

{2} Biomolecules: The Chemicals of Life.................................7

Chapter 2 Quiz.................................9

Unit 1 Exam.................................13

UNIT 2

{3} A Short History of Microscopy.................................19

Chapter 3 Quiz.................................21

{4} Introduction to Cell Basics.................................23

Chapter 4 Quiz.................................25

{5} Organelles of the Eukaryotic Cell.................................27

Chapter 5 Quiz.................................29

Unit 2 Exam.................................31

UNIT 3

{6} Basics of Metabolism.................................35

Chapter 6 Quiz.................................37

{7}   Photosynthesis: Building Plants out of Thin Air 39

       Chapter 7 Quiz 41

{8}   Cellular Respiration: Making Food into Thin Air. 43

       Chapter 8 Quiz 45

       Unit 3 Exam. 47

UNIT 4

{9}   The Central Dogma: DNA and How It Codes for Proteins. 51

       Chapter 9 Quiz 53

{10} The Lac Operon: How Genes are Turned Off and On 57

       Chapter 10 Quiz 59

{11} Recombinant DNA Technology and Genetic Modification 61

       Chapter 11 Quiz 63

       Unit 4 Exam. 65

UNIT 5

{12} Mitosis and Cell Division 69

       Chapter 12 Quiz 71

{13} Meiosis. 73

       Chapter 13 Quiz 75

{14} The Basics of Mendelian Genetics. 77

       Chapter 14 Quiz 79

       Unit 5 Exam. 83

       Part 1 Comprehensive Exam 89

PART 2: DIVERSITY OF LIFE

UNIT 6

{15} Classifying Life. 97
    Chapter 15 Quiz 99

{16} The Viruses and Prokaryotes 101
    Chapter 16 Quiz 103

{17} The Algae: Plant-like Protists 105
    Chapter 17 Quiz 107

    Unit 6 Exam. 109

UNIT 7

{18} Animal-like and Fungal-like Protists. 115
    Chapter 18 Quiz 117

{19} Kingdom Fungi. 119
    Chapter 19 Quiz 121

{20} Kingdom Animalia: A Short Introduction. 123
    Chapter 20 Quiz 125

    Unit 7 Exam. 127

UNIT 8

{21} Phylum Porifera: The Sponges. 133
    Chapter 21 Quiz 135

{22} Phylum Cnidaria: Jellyfish, Sea Anemones, Coral, Etc.. 137
    Chapter 22 Quiz 139

{23} The Worms. 141
    Chapter 23 Quiz 143

    Unit 8 Exam. 147

UNIT 9

{24} Phylum Mollusca: The Mollusks—Clams, Oysters, Snails, Slugs, Squid, Etc. 153

Chapter 24 Quiz 155

{25} Phylum Arthropoda: The Arthropods—Crustaceans, Arachnids, Insects, Etc. 157

Chapter 25 Quiz 159

{26} Phylum Echinodermata: The Echinoderms 163

Chapter 26 Quiz 165

Unit 9 Exam 167

UNIT 10

{27} Phylum Chordata: The Chordates 175

Chapter 27 Quiz 177

{28} Kingdom Plantae: Plants 181

Chapter 28 Quiz 183

{29} The Basics of Ecology 187

Chapter 29 Quiz 189

Unit 10 Exam 191

Part 2 Comprehensive Exam 199

Quiz and Exam Answer Key 207

PART 1

THE LIVING CELL

A SMIDGE *of* CHEMISTRY

OBJECTIVES

1. Know the definitions of atom, element, molecule, compound, atomic number, atomic weight, isotope, ion (cation and anion), salt, and buffer. Be able to give examples.

2. Know the three subatomic particles of an atom, their location, and charge.

3. Given the atomic number of an element be able to draw a simple diagram of one of its atoms with electrons properly distributed in their shells and orbitals.

4. Know the definitions of the three types (and sub-types) of chemical bonds and their relative strengths. Be able to draw each kind of bond using the examples given in the book.

5. Know the properties of water.

6. Know the pH scale and what it is a measure of. Know what is considered neutral pH, the acidic range, and the basic (alkaline) range. If there is a change of one pH unit, know how much more or less acidic it is.

 Thoroughly study the above objectives before you take the chapter quiz. Be sure you know how to spell the terms.

CHAPTER 1 QUIZ

1. A substance that has distinct chemical properties and cannot be broken down into simpler substances by normal chemical means is a(n)_____.

2. The smallest unit of an element is a(n) _____.

3. A molecule containing two or more elements is a(n) _____.

4. The two subatomic particles contained in the nucleus of an atom are _____ and _____. What are their charges? (place the appropriate charge next to each name)

5. The subatomic particles contained in the shells orbiting the nucleus are the _____. Charge? _____

6. Atomic number is the number of _____.

7. Draw an oxygen atom (atomic number: 8).

8. Draw a water molecule (H_2O) showing orbitals and shared electrons (atomic number of hydrogen: 1).

9. A complete transfer of electrons from one atom to another resulting in oppositely charged atoms sticking together is called a(n) _____ bond.

10. When atoms are joined together because they are sharing electrons it is called a(n) _____ bond.

11. In a _____ covalent bond electrons are unevenly shared whereas in a _____ covalent bond electrons are evenly shared.

12. Weak attractions between partially positively charged atoms and partially negatively charged atoms within the same molecule or between different molecules are called _____ bonds.

13. The pH scale is a measure of a substance's _____ ion concentration.

14. A move from pH 6 to pH 5 has made the solution _____ times more acidic.

    a. 2

    b. 5

    c. 10

    d. 100

15. Substances that resist changes in pH are called _____.

BIOMOLECULES

THE CHEMICALS OF LIFE

OBJECTIVES

1. Know the four major categories of biomolecules and the sub-categories of each.

2. Know the "TinkerToy" rules for the major elements of life; i.e., carbon, hydrogen, oxygen, nitrogen, phosphorus, and sulfur.

3. Know the building blocks (and how to draw them) of the four major categories of biomolecules. Carbohydrates—monosaccharide (glucose); Lipids—glycerol and fatty acid; be able to draw a stick figure of a phospholipid and be able to recognize a cholesterol molecule; Proteins—amino acids; Nucleic acids—be able to draw a stick figure of a nucleotide.

4. Know how to draw either a dehydration synthesis or hydrolysis reaction between two monosaccharides, between a glycerol and a fatty acid, or between two amino acids. Know how to connect stick figures of nucleotides together.

5. Know how to draw a phospholipid bilayer.

6. Know the relationship between the amino acid sequence in a protein and the function of a protein.

7. Know the basic functions of the four major categories of biomolecules.

 Thoroughly study the above objectives before you take the chapter quiz. Be sure you know how to spell the terms. Study hard for this chapter. You'll need lots of practice drawing these biomolecules.

CHAPTER 2 QUIZ

1. What are the 'TinkerToy rules' (how many bonds does it usually form with other atoms) for the following?

    a. Carbon _____

    b. Hydrogen _____

    c. Oxygen _____

    d. Nitrogen _____

    e. Phosphorus _____

    f. Sulfur _____

2. Name the four major biomolecule categories.

    a. _____

    b. _____

    c. _____

    d. _____

3. Name one example of a disaccharide. _____

4. Cellulose is one type of _____.

5. Give one function of cellulose: _____

6. Draw glucose doing a dehydration synthesis reaction with another glucose forming a disaccharide. Label the glycosidic linkage.

7.   Draw a glycerol doing a dehydration synthesis reaction with a fatty acid (4 carbons long) to form a monoglyceride.

8.   Draw a short section of a phospholipid bilayer (using stick figure phospholipids).

9.   Draw an amino acid doing a dehydration synthesis reaction with another amino acid to form a dipeptide. Label the peptide bond.

10. A chain of 100 or more amino acids is called a _____.

11. A chain of 60 amino acids is called a _____.

12. Draw a stick figure of a nucleotide and label its three components.

13. The sequence of amino acids determines the _____ of the

    protein, which in turn determines the _____ of the protein.

14. Name five different types of jobs done by proteins.

    a. _____

    b. _____

    c. _____

    d. _____

    e. _____

15. Name two functions of nucleotides other than storing genetic information.

    a. _____

    b. _____

    ✳ **Study all the objectives for this unit. Make sure you know the correct answers for the quizzes. Understand the concepts and terms; don't just memorize them. Then take the Unit Exam.**

UNIT 1 EXAM

1. A substance that has distinct chemical properties and cannot be broken down into simpler substances by normal chemical means is a(n) _____ .

2. The smallest unit of an element is a(n) _____ .

3. A molecule containing two or more elements is a(n) _____ .

4. The two subatomic particles contained in the nucleus of an atom are _____ and _____ . Place the appropriate charge next to each name.

5. The subatomic particles contained in the shells orbiting the nucleus are the _____ . Place their charge next to the name.

6. Atomic number is the number of _____ .

7. Atomic weight is the number of protons and _____ .

8. Draw an oxygen atom (atomic number: 8).

9. Draw a water molecule (H_2O) showing orbitals and shared electrons (atomic number of hydrogen: 1).

10. A complete transfer of electrons from one atom to another resulting in oppositely charged atoms sticking together is called a(n) _____ bond.

11. When atoms are joined together because they are sharing electrons it is called a(n) _____ bond.

12. In a _____ covalent bond electrons are unevenly shared, whereas in a _____ covalent bond electrons are evenly shared.

13. Weak attractions between partially positive charged atoms and partially negative charged atoms within the same molecule or between different molecules are called _____ bonds.

14. The pH scale is a measure of a substance's _____ ion concentration.

15. A pH of 7 is termed _____. Below pH 7 is considered _____ and above 7 is considered _____.

16. A move from pH 6 to pH 5 has made the solution _____ times more acidic.

    a. 2
    b. 5
    c. 10
    d. 100

17. Substances that resist changes in pH are called _____.

18. What are the 'TinkerToy rules' (how many bonds does it usually form with other atoms) for the following?

    a. Carbon _____
    b. Hydrogen _____
    c. Oxygen _____
    d. Nitrogen _____
    e. Phosphorus _____
    f. Sulfur _____

19. Name the four major biomolecule categories.

    a. _____

    b. _____

    c. _____

    d. _____

20. Name one example of a disaccharide. _____

21. Cellulose is one type of _____.

22. Give one function of cellulose. _____.

23. Draw glucose doing a dehydration synthesis reaction with another glucose forming a disaccharide. Label the glycosidic linkage.

24. Draw a glycerol doing a dehydration synthesis reaction with a fatty acid (4 carbons long) to form a monoglyceride.

25. Draw a short section of a phospholipid bilayer (using stick figure phospholipids).

26. Draw an amino acid doing a dehydration synthesis reaction with another amino acid to form a dipeptide. Label the peptide bond.

27. A chain of 100 or more amino acids is called a _____.

28. A chain of 60 amino acids is called a _____.

29. Draw a stick figure of a nucleotide and label its three components.

30. The sequence of amino acids determines the _____ of the protein, which in turn determines the _____ of the protein.

31. Name five different types of jobs done by proteins.

    a. _____

    b. _____

    c. _____

    d. _____

    e. _____

32. Name two functions of nucleotides other than storing genetic information.

    a. _____

    b. _____

A SHORT HISTORY *of* MICROSCOPY

OBJECTIVES

1. Know the contributions of the following people and the century in which they made their contributions.

   - Galileo
   - Francesco Stelluti
   - Robert Hooke
   - Antony van Leeuwenhoek

2. Know the three tenets of the Cell Theory, the men who proposed it, and the century they did their work.

 Thoroughly study the above objectives before you take the chapter quiz. Be sure you know how to spell the terms.

CHAPTER 3 QUIZ

1. What other invention was closely associated with the microscope?

    _____

2. Who was the English scientist who coined the term cell?

    _____

3. What Latin word is cell derived from? _____

4. Why did Hooke pick that term? _____

    _____

5. Who was the Dutchman who viewed microscopic life with a microscope of his own making? _____

6. What did he call these life forms? _____

7. In what century did he make these observations? _____

8. Were Hooke and Leeuwenhoek contemporaries? _____

9. What are the three tenets of the Cell Theory?

    a. _____
    b. _____
    c. _____

10. Who were the three men who composed this theory?

    a. _____
    b. _____
    c. _____

INTRODUCTION *to* CELL BASICS

OBJECTIVES

1. Know the basic differences between the prokaryotic and eukaryotic cells and know the life forms that are composed of these cell types.

2. Understand the main reasons why most cells need to be very small. Know two problems that arise if cells were too large.

3. Be able to label phospholipids and proteins in a diagram of the fluid mosaic model of a cell membrane.

4. Know the definitions of solvent, solute, solution, diffusion.

5. Know how temperature, concentration, and molecular size affect diffusion rates.

6. Know the relationship between diffusion and Brownian motion.

7. Know the definition of osmosis, plasmolysis, cytolysis, hemolysis, and turgor pressure.

8. Understand the concept of tonicity. Know what happens to cells placed in solutions having the following tonicities: hypertonic, hypotonic, and isotonic.

9. Be able to describe the following processes:
   - Simple diffusion
   - Passive transport or facilitated diffusion
   - Active transport
   - Endocytosis and the difference between the two types
   - Exocytosis

Thoroughly study the above objectives before you take the chapter quiz. Be sure you know how to spell the terms.

CHAPTER 4 QUIZ

1. How do prokaryotic cells differ from eukaryotic cells regarding:

    a. A nucleus? _____

    b. Organelles? _____

    c. Size? _____

2. If a cell is too big what becomes too small relative to the increased mass?

    _____

3. Using stick figures for phospholipids and blob-like shapes for proteins; draw a small section of a biological membrane.

4. Define diffusion: _____

    _____

5. What fundamental property of matter causes diffusion?

    _____

6. How does concentration affect diffusion rate?

    _____

7. Define osmosis: _____

    _____

8. If a plant cell is placed in a hypertonic solution, it will _____ (lose/gain) water. This condition is called _____.

    When this occurs what happens to the turgor pressure?

    _____

9.   Movement of a substance across a membrane, through a protein gate but against a concentration gradient is called _____.

10.   The engulfing of a food particle by a cell so that a food vacuole is formed within the cell containing the food is _____.

CHAPTER 5

ORGANELLES
OF THE EUKARYOTIC CELL

OBJECTIVES

1. Know what cytoplasm is.

2. Identify the eukaryotic organelles and describe their functions.

3. Know the different types of cytoskeletal elements and their functions.

4. Know the roles different extracellular materials play in various organisms.

5. Know the different cell-to-cell junctions and their basic function.

 Thoroughly study the above objectives before you take the chapter quiz. Be sure you know how to spell the terms.

CHAPTER 5 QUIZ

1. The _____ contains the vast majority of DNA.

2. The _____ within the [answer to #1] is a site where certain components of ribosomes are made.

3. _____ are tiny organelles used in the construction of proteins.

4. The _____ is covered with ribosomes and is involved in the modification of newly made proteins.

5. The _____ is devoid of ribosomes and is mostly involved with the manufacture or remodeling of _____.

6. The fluid of the cell is called the _____ and is 80 to 95% _____.

7. The organelle that "burns" food to make ATP for the cells' energy needs is the _____.

8. The organelle that captures sunlight energy to make glucose out of carbon dioxide and water is the _____.

9. The organelle involved in modifying, packaging, and shipping various biomolecules to other organelles or the cell membrane is the

   _____.

10. If an ameba phagocytosed bacteria, the resulting vesicle within the cell is called a _____.

11. An organelle that contains digestive enzymes for the demolition of various biomolecules is the _____.

12. Various proteins that form internal 'tent poles' or form internal transport rails or form parts to molecular motors are called _____ elements.

13. One type of the above that form the inner framework and motor apparatus contained in flagella and cilia are _____.

14. The rigid to flexible supporting framework outside the cell membrane of plant, fungi, and bacterial cells is called the _____.

15. Cell-to-cell junctions that actually allow cytoplasm to flow between adjacent cells are called _____ junctions.

 Study all the objectives for this unit. Make sure you know the correct answers for the quizzes. Understand the concepts and terms; don't just memorize them. Then take the Unit Exam.

UNIT 2 EXAM

1.   What other invention was closely associated with the microscope?

     _____

2.   The first publication of microscope illustrations was done by

     _____.

     The creatures drawn were _____.

3.   Who was the English scientist who coined the term cell?

     _____

4.   What Latin word is cell derived from? _____

5.   Why did Hooke pick that term? _____

     _____

6.   Who was the Dutchman who viewed microscopic life with a microscope of

     his own making? _____

7.   What did he call these life forms? _____

8.   What century did he make these observations? _____

9.   Were Hooke and Leeuwenhoek contemporaries? _____

10. What are the three tenets of the Cell Theory?

     a. _____

     b. _____

     c. _____

11. Who were the three men who composed this theory?

     a. _____   b. _____

     c. _____

12. How do prokaryotic cells differ from eukaryotic cells regarding:

    a. A nucleus? _____

    b. Organelles? _____

    c. Size? _____

13. If a cell is too big what becomes too small relative to the increased mass?

    _____

14. Using stick figures for phospholipids and blob-like shapes for proteins; draw a small section of a biological membrane.

15. Define diffusion: _____

    _____

16. What fundamental property of matter causes diffusion?

    _____

17. How does concentration affect diffusion rate? _____

    _____

18. How does temperature affect diffusion rate? _____

    _____

19. How does molecular size affect diffusion rate? _____

    _____

20. Define osmosis: _____

    _____

21. If a plant cell is placed in a hypertonic solution, it will _____
    (lose/gain) water. This condition is called _____.
    When this occurs what happens to the turgor pressure? _____
    _____

22. Movement of a substance across a membrane, through a protein gate but
    against a concentration gradient is called _____.

23. The engulfing of a food particle by a cell so that a food vacuole is formed
    within the cell containing the food is _____.

24. The _____ contains the vast majority of DNA.

25. The _____ within the [answer to #24] is a
    site where certain components of ribosomes are made.

26. _____ are tiny organelles used in the
    construction of proteins.

27. The _____ is covered with ribosomes and is
    involved in the modification of newly made _____.

28. The _____ is devoid of ribosomes and is mostly
    involved with the manufacture or remodeling of _____.

29. The fluid of the cell is called the _____ and
    is 80 to 95% _____.

30. The organelle that 'burns' food to make ATP for the cells' energy needs is the
    _____.

31. The organelle that captures sunlight energy to make glucose out of carbon
    dioxide and water is the _____.

32. The organelle involved in modifying, packaging, and shipping various biomolecules to other organelles or the cell membrane is the

_____.

33. If an ameba phagocytosed bacteria, the resulting vesicle within the cell is called a _____.

34. An organelle that contains digestive enzymes for the demolition of various biomolecules is the _____.

35. Various proteins that form internal 'tent poles' or form internal transport rails or form parts to molecular motors are called _____ elements.

36. One type of the above that form the inner framework and motor apparatus contained in flagella and cilia are _____.

37. The rigid to flexible supporting framework outside the cell membrane of plant, fungi, and bacterial cells is called the _____.

38. Cell-to-cell junctions that actually allow cytoplasm to flow between adjacent cells are called _____ junctions.

BASICS *of* METABOLISM

OBJECTIVES

1. Understand what natural law is from a Christian perspective.

2. Understand and be able to simply describe the First and Second Law of Thermodynamics.

3. Be able to label the symbols of reactants and products in a reaction equation.

4. Be able to describe the difference between endergonic and exergonic reactions and other reactions that can be categorized under these two.

5. Define metabolism, enzymes, active site, substrate, denaturation, allosteric site, and allosteric inhibition.

6. Be able to draw a simple cartoon of a substrate binding to an enzyme.

7. Know and understand how temperature, pH, and enzyme concentration can affect enzyme activity.

8. Know the two main groups of enzyme helpers.

 Thoroughly study the above objectives before you take the chapter quiz. Be sure you know how to spell the terms.

CHAPTER 6 QUIZ

1. The law that states that matter cannot be created or destroyed but can be converted from one form to another is the _____ _____.

2. Contrast anabolic and catabolic reactions. _____

   _____

   _____

   _____

3. Which one above is endergonic? _____

4. Using A, B, and C show a catabolic reaction in symbolic form.

5. Proteins that speed up chemical reactions millions of times faster are called _____.

6. Name three things that affect enzyme activity.

   a. _____

   b. _____

   c. _____

7. Denaturation deforms or destroys the enzyme's _____.

8. Enzymes convert substrates into _____ using their active sites.

9. The sum total of all the chemical reactions in cells, tissues, or the entire body is called _____.

10. Heavy metals can act as poisons by binding to the enzyme's
_____ site. This deforms the active
site which destroys enzyme function.

PHOTOSYNTHESIS

BUILDING PLANTS OUT OF THIN AIR

OBJECTIVES

1. Know the general equation for photosynthesis.

2. Be able to describe a zoom down from the macro scale of the leaf to the micro scale of the chloroplast.

3. Be able to draw a simple sketch of a chloroplast and label the parts.

4. Know how the ingredients (CO_2 and H_2O) of photosynthesis get to the chloroplasts and how the product glucose is transported and used by the plant. Also know where the oxygen goes as a waste product.

5. Know the location and the two products of the light dependent reactions.

6. Know the details of how those two products are made as a result of the ETS (Electron Transport System). Be able to explain these processes using analogies given in the text. Know what kind of energy drives the electron flow in the ETS, the role of the chlorophylls and antenna pigments within the photosystems, and the compound that serves as the electron source. Know what oxidation and reduction is in the context of the ETS.

7. Know the location and product of the light independent reactions (Calvin-Benson Cycle). Know the acronyms of each intermediate in the Calvin-Benson Cycle.

8. Know some of the many biomolecules of plants that can trace their beginnings to glucose.

 Thoroughly study the above objectives before you take the chapter quiz. Be sure you know how to spell the terms.

CHAPTER 7 QUIZ

1. What is the general equation of photosynthesis?

    _____

2. CO_2 enters the leaf through the _____.

3. O_2 leaves the leaf through the _____.

4. Draw and label a chloroplast.

5. The photosynthetic pigments are in two clusters called _____
    and _____.

6. The major pigment that captures light energy and drives the electron
    transport system in the chloroplasts is _____.

7. Other photosystem pigments that capture a wider range of wavelengths of light
    and transfer that energy to chlorophyll are the _____
    pigments.

8. These pigments along with the electron transport system move electrons from
    _____ (the ultimate electron source) to
    _____.

9. What is a product of photosynthesis resulting from water being stripped of some
    of its electrons by Photosystem II? _____

10. What type of energy excites chlorophyll causing electrons to flow through the ETS? _____

11. What accumulates inside the thylakoid discs when they are receiving light? _____.

12. ATP is generated from ADP and P when _____ ions flow through a channel protein/enzyme called _____.

13. What are the two important products of the Light Dependent Reactions?

     a. _____

     b. _____

14. The cycle that produces glucose from CO_2 is called the _____ cycle. This cycle is considered the Light _____ Reactions.

15. The Light Dependent Reactions occur in the _____ membrane but the Light Independent Reactions occur in the _____ _____.

CELLULAR RESPIRATION
MAKING FOOD INTO THIN AIR

OBJECTIVES

1. Know the general equation for cellular respiration and compare its products with the reactants of photosynthesis. Of cellular respiration and photosynthesis know which one is endergonic and which one is exergonic.

2. Know the starting (glucose) and ending molecules (pyruvates) of glycolysis. Know where glycolysis occurs and know the quantities of the two important products (NADH and ATP) after glycolysis.

3. Know how pyruvates are broken down into CO_2 (oxidized) in the mitochondria (acetyl CoA formation and the Krebs Cycle). Know the quantities of NADH, $FADH_2$, and ATP for each pyruvate broken down.

4. Be able to draw and label a mitochondrion.

5. Be able to describe how CO_2 is released from the intermediate molecules in these reactions.

6. Know the function of NADH and $FADH_2$ and how they are utilized by the ETS in the mitochondria. Know the purpose of the ETS in the mitochondria. Be able to explain the causal link between NADH/$FADH_2$ and ATP production. Compare it with ATP production in photosynthesis.

7. Know the final electron acceptor (oxygen) in the ETS of the mitochondria and be able to explain what happens when it is not available.

8. Know the grand total yield of ATP by oxidizing one molecule of glucose.

9. Understand the big picture of cellular respiration.

 Thoroughly study the above objectives before you take the chapter quiz. Be sure you know how to spell the terms.

CHAPTER 8 QUIZ

1.   The *net* production of ATP in glycolysis only is _____.

2.   Glycolysis occurs in the _____.

3.   The _____ cycle generates the most NADH.

4.   In glycolysis, glucose is ultimately split (by oxidation) into two

      _____.

5.   The NADH yield for glycolysis is _____.

6.   In cellular respiration the Electron Transport System occurs in the

      _____ membrane of the mitochondrion.

7.   Draw and label a mitochondrion.

8.   In the mitochondria what two molecules release (dump) their electrons onto
      the Electron Transport System?

      a. _____

      b. _____

9.   How much ATP does one NADH generate when using the ETS? _____

10.   What ions are pumped out into the intermembrane space of the
      mitochondrion as electrons zip through the Electron Transport System?

      _____

11. Phosphorylation (ADP + P → ATP) occurs when

    _____ ions flow through a channel

    protein/enzyme called _____.

12. How many NADHs are produced (total) when burning one molecule of

    glucose (from glucose to CO_2)? _____

13. In cellular respiration what important molecule from the air does all aerobic

    life need, that accepts electrons (and hydrogen) at the end of the Electron

    Transport System? _____

14. What happens to ATP production if [the answer to #13] is unavailable?

    _____

15. What is the grand total ATP yield from burning one molecule of glucose into

    $6CO_2$ and $6H_2O$? _____

  Study all the objectives for this unit. Make sure you know the
correct answers for the quizzes. Understand the concepts and
terms; don't just memorize them. Then take the Unit Exam.

UNIT 3 EXAM

1. The law that states that matter cannot be created or destroyed but can be converted from one form to another is the _____

   _____ .

2. Contrast anabolic and catabolic reactions: _____

   _____

   _____

3. Which one above is endergonic? _____

4. Using the letters A, B, and C show a catabolic reaction in symbolic form.

5. Proteins that speed up chemical reactions millions of times faster are called

   _____ .

6. Name three things that affect enzyme activity.

   a. _____

   b. _____

   c. _____

7. Denaturation deforms or destroys the enzyme's _____ .

8. Enzymes convert substrates into _____
   using their active sites.

9. The sum total of all the chemical reactions in cells, tissues, or the entire body
   is called _____ .

10. Heavy metals can act as poisons by binding to the enzyme's
    _____ site. This deforms the active site
    which destroys enzyme function.

11. What is the general equation of photosynthesis?

    _____

12. CO_2 enters the leaf through the _____.

13. O_2 leaves the leaf through the _____.

14. Draw and label a chloroplast.

15. The photosynthetic pigments are in two clusters called
    _____ and _____.

16. The major pigment that captures light energy and drives the electron
    transport system in the chloroplasts is _____.

17. Other photosystem pigments that capture a wider range of
    wavelengths of light and transfer that energy to chlorophyll are the
    _____ pigments.

18. These pigments along with the electron transport system move electrons
    from _____ (the ultimate electron source) to
    _____.

19. What is a product of photosynthesis resulting from water being stripped of some
    of its electrons by Photosystem II? _____

20. What type of energy excites chlorophyll causing electrons to flow through the ETS? _____

21. What accumulates inside the thylakoid discs when they are receiving light? _____.

22. ATP is generated from ADP and P when _____ ions flow through a channel protein/enzyme called _____ _____.

23. What are the two important products of the Light Dependent Reactions?

    a. _____

    b. _____

24. The cycle that produces glucose from CO_2 is called the _____ cycle. This cycle is considered the Light _____ Reactions.

25. The Light Dependent Reactions occur in the _____ membrane but the Light Independent Reactions (Calvin-Benson cycle) occur in the _____.

26. The *net* production of ATP in glycolysis only is _____.

27. Glycolysis occurs in the _____.

28. The _____ cycle generates the most NADH.

29. In glycolysis, glucose is ultimately split (by oxidation) into two _____.

30. The NADH yield for glycolysis is _____.

31. In cellular respiration the Electron Transport System occurs in the _____ membrane of the mitochondrion.

32. Draw and label a mitochondrion.

33. In the mitochondria what two molecules release (dump) their electrons onto the Electron Transport System?

    a. _____

    b. _____

34. How much ATP does one NADH generate when using the ETS? _____

35. What ions are pumped out into the intermembrane space of the mitochondrion as electrons zip through the Electron Transport System?

    _____

36. Phosphorylation (ADP + P → ATP) occurs when _____ ions flow through a channel protein/enzyme called _____ .

37. How many NADHs are produced (total) when burning one molecule of glucose (from glucose to CO_2)? _____

38. In cellular respiration what important molecule from the air does all aerobic life need, that accepts electrons (and hydrogen) at the end of the Electron Transport System? _____

39. What happens to ATP production if [the answer to #38] is unavailable?

    _____

40. What is the grand total ATP yield from burning one molecule of glucose into $6CO_2$ and $6H_2O$? _____

 CENTRAL DOGMA: DNA
AND HOW IT CODES FOR PROTEINS

OBJECTIVES

1. Know the discoverers of DNA's structure.

2. Be able to identify the five different nitrogenous bases and know their position in a nucleotide. Know which ones are purines and pyrimidines.

3. Know the base pairing rules.

4. Know how nucleotides are arranged to form a nucleic acid.

5. Know the differences between DNA and RNA.

6. Know the various levels of coiling (the ones named in the text) in the chromosome's structure.

7. Be able to draw and label the central dogma diagram.

8. Be able to describe RNA transcription, the name and function of its key enzyme, and where it occurs.

9. Be able to describe Protein translation. Know where it occurs, the role of the ribosome, and the functions of the different types of RNAs.

10. Given a base sequence of a length of DNA be able to construct the RNA sequence that would have been produced by RNA transcription. From the RNA sequence, be able to group the bases into codons. Lastly, by using the genetic code table, be able to figure out the amino acid sequence of the polypeptide or protein.

11. Be able to state a big problem in assuming that the central dogma evolved without a Creator.

 Thoroughly study the above objectives before you take the chapter quiz. Be sure you know how to spell the terms.

CHAPTER 9 QUIZ

1. Who were the two main discoverers (full names) of the structure of DNA?

    a. _____

    b. _____

2. Who also won the Nobel Prize with them?

    _____

3. The data that was the most valuable to this discovery was generated by two scientists named _____

    and _____ (full names).

4. What are the three parts to a nucleotide?

    a. _____

    b. _____

    c. _____

5. What are the four different nitrogenous bases found in DNA?

    a. _____

    b. _____

    c. _____

    d. _____

6. The double helix can be likened to a twisted ladder. The "ladder sides" are called the _____ backbones and the "rungs" are the base-pairs.

7. In a chromosome, DNA is neatly wrapped around proteins called histones forming little repeating spools called _____ .

8. The enzyme that unzips the two parental strands of DNA apart and constructs a complementary strand of RNA is called _____.

9. Name three structural differences between RNA and DNA nucleotides.

    a. _____

    b. _____

    c. _____

10. If a DNA strand is T-A-C-G-C-G-C-T-T-G-A-T-T-T-A, what is the mRNA sequence? (Put a slash between codons)

    _____

11. What is the amino acid sequence? (Use the three letter abbreviations for the amino acids; refer to the following genetic code.) _____

FIRST BASE	SECOND BASE				THIRD BASE
	U	C	A	G	
U	Phe	Ser	Tyr	Cys	U
	Phe	Ser	Tyr	Cys	C
	Leu	Ser	STOP	STOP	A
	Leu	Ser	STOP	Trp	G
C	Leu	Pro	His	Arg	U
	Leu	Pro	His	Arg	C
	Leu	Pro	Gln	Arg	A
	Leu	Pro	Gln	Arg	G
A	Ile	Thr	Asn	Ser	U
	Ile	Thr	Asn	Ser	C
	Ile	Thr	Lys	Arg	A
	Met	Thr	Lys	Arg	G
G	Val	Ala	Asp	Gly	U
	Val	Ala	Asp	Gly	C
	Val	Ala	Glu	Gly	A
	Val	Ala	Glu	Gly	G

12. When protein is made from an mRNA transcript, the process is called

_____.

13. What molecule contains the anticodon and retrieves the appropriate amino acid?

_____

14. True or false? Portions of RNA are snipped out (i.e., edited out) and the remaining pieces are spliced together before translation occurs.

15. What is the fundamental problem for those who think the central dogma evolved without a creator? _____

 LAC OPERON

HOW GENES ARE TURNED OFF AND ON

OBJECTIVES

1. Know the discoverers of the lac operon. Also know the organism they discovered it in.

2. Be able to describe how the lac operon works and the logic behind it.

 Thoroughly study the above objectives before you take the chapter quiz. Be sure you know how to spell the terms.

CHAPTER 10 QUIZ

1. Who were the two biologists that discovered the lac operon?

   _____ and _____

2. What organism is the lac operon in? _____

3. What protein attaches to the operator to prevent certain genes from being transcribed in the lac operon? _____

4. What is the place on DNA to which RNA polymerase attaches at the beginning of transcription? _____

5. A gene or a set of genes that are turned on or off by a single switch is called a(n) _____.

6. In the lac operon, lactose binds to the _____ which causes it to fall off the operator.

7. If this binding occurs, name the first enzyme that is made (translated)?

   _____

8. What does this enzyme do? _____

9. What is the second enzyme made and what does it do?

   _____

   _____

10. What happens to the repressor if all the lactose is consumed?

   _____

   _____

CHAPTER II

RECOMBINANT DNA TECHNOLOGY
AND GENETIC MODIFICATION

OBJECTIVES

1. Know functions of restriction enzymes and DNA ligase.

2. Know what plasmids and sticky ends are.

3. Be able to describe all the steps in recombinant DNA technology. Also know how the above are used in recombinant DNA technology.

4. Know how antibiotic resistance genes are used to identify those cells that were transformed.

5. Know the basic idea behind the following methods of DNA acquisition: transformation, transduction, conjugation, and bioballistics.

6. Be able to describe how recombinant DNA technology was used in the three examples mentioned in the text.

 Thoroughly study the above objectives before you take the chapter quiz. Be sure you know how to spell the terms.

CHAPTER 11 QUIZ

1. Enzymes used to cut DNA at specific sequences are called
    _____ enzymes.

2. The enzyme used to splice DNA fragments together is called
    _____.

3. Overhanging ends of single-stranded DNA which facilitate the splicing
    process are called _____.

4. After a *gene of interest* is spliced into a plasmid, what must be done next in
    order to put the gene to work? _____

5. What mode of DNA acquisition involves a virus as a vehicle to inject DNA
    into the cell? _____

6. What mode of DNA acquisition involves shooting microscopic DNA-coated
    metal particles into the cell? _____

7. What mode of DNA acquisition is from a bacterium to another bacterium
    through pilus? _____

8. List the seven basic steps in recombinant DNA technology.

    a. _____

    b. _____

    c. _____

    d. _____

    e. _____

    f. _____

    g. _____

9. The gene that codes for _____ was successfully inserted into a plasmid. *E. coli* was transformed with the plasmid and can now produce large quantities of this hormone for the treatment of diabetes.

10. *Agrobacterium tumefaciens* can be used to deliver beneficial genes to crops. What must be removed from the Ti plasmid for it to work without harming the plant? _____

 Study all the objectives for this unit. Make sure you know the correct answers for the quizzes. Understand the concepts and terms; don't just memorize them. Then take the Unit Exam.

UNIT 4 EXAM

1. Who were the two main discoverers (full names) of the structure of DNA?

   a. _____

   b. _____

2. Who also won the Nobel Prize with them?

   _____

3. The data that was the most valuable to this discovery was generated by two scientists named _____ and _____ (full names).

4. What are the three parts to a nucleotide?

   a. _____

   b. _____

   c. _____

5. What are the four different nitrogenous bases found in DNA?

   a. _____

   b. _____

   c. _____

   d. _____

6. The double helix can be likened to a twisted ladder. The "ladder sides" are called the _____ backbones and the "rungs" are the base-pairs.

7. In a chromosome, DNA is neatly wrapped around proteins called histones forming little repeating spools called _____.

8. The enzyme that unzips the two parental strands of DNA apart and constructs a complementary strand of RNA is called _____.

9. Name three structural differences between RNA and DNA.

    a. _____

    b. _____

    c. _____

10. If a DNA strand is T-A-C-G-C-G-C-T-T-G-A-T-T-T-A, what is the mRNA sequence? (Put a slash between codons)

    _____

11. What is the amino acid sequence? (Use the three letter abbreviations for the amino acids; refer to the following genetic code.) _____

FIRST BASE	SECOND BASE				THIRD BASE
	U	C	A	G	
U	Phe	Ser	Tyr	Cys	U
	Phe	Ser	Tyr	Cys	C
	Leu	Ser	STOP	STOP	A
	Leu	Ser	STOP	Trp	G
C	Leu	Pro	His	Arg	U
	Leu	Pro	His	Arg	C
	Leu	Pro	Gln	Arg	A
	Leu	Pro	Gln	Arg	G
A	Ile	Thr	Asn	Ser	U
	Ile	Thr	Asn	Ser	C
	Ile	Thr	Lys	Arg	A
	Met	Thr	Lys	Arg	G
G	Val	Ala	Asp	Gly	U
	Val	Ala	Asp	Gly	C
	Val	Ala	Glu	Gly	A
	Val	Ala	Glu	Gly	G

12. When protein is made from an mRNA transcript, the process is called

    _____

13. What molecule contains the anticodon and retrieves the appropriate amino acid?

    _____

14. What is the fundamental problem for those who think the central dogma evolved without a creator?

    _____

15. Who were the two biologists that discovered the lac operon?

    _____ and _____

16. What organism is the lac operon in? _____

17. What protein attaches to the operator to prevent certain genes from being transcribed in the lac operon? _____

18. What is the place on DNA to which RNA polymerase attaches at the beginning of transcription? _____

19. A gene or a set of genes that are turned on or off by a single switch is called a(n)

    _____ .

20. In the lac operon, lactose binds to the _____ which causes it to fall off the operator.

21. If this binding occurs, name the first enzyme that is made (translated)?

    _____

22. What does this enzyme do? _____

23. What is the second enzyme made and what does it do?

    _____

24. What happens to the repressor if all the lactose is consumed?

    _____

    _____

25. Enzymes used to cut DNA at specific sequences are called
    _____ enzymes.

26. The enzyme used to splice DNA fragments together is called
    _____.

27. Overhanging ends of single-stranded DNA which facilitate the splicing
    process are called _____.

28. After a *gene of interest* is spliced into a plasmid, what must be done next in
    order to put the gene to work? _____

29. What mode of DNA acquisition involves a virus as a vehicle to inject DNA
    into the cell? _____

30. What mode of DNA acquisition involves shooting microscopic DNA-coated
    metal particles into the cell? _____

31. What mode of DNA acquisition is from a bacterium to another bacterium
    through pilus? _____

32. List the seven basic steps in recombinant DNA technology.

    a. _____
    b. _____
    c. _____
    d. _____
    e. _____
    f. _____
    g. _____

33. The gene that codes for _____ was
    successfully inserted into a plasmid. *E. coli* was transformed with the plasmid and
    can now produce large quantities of this hormone for the treatment of diabetes.

MITOSIS AND CELL DIVISION

OBJECTIVES

1. Know the logic behind mitosis.

2. Be able to describe the process of DNA replication and why it needs to occur before mitosis.

3. Know what's happening during the three phases of interphase.

4. Be able to describe what's happening in each phase of mitosis and why. In describing mitosis, be able to use any boldface terminology that is mentioned in the process.

5. Be able to describe both plant and animal cytokinesis highlighting how they differ from each other.

 Thoroughly study the above objectives before you take the chapter quiz. Be sure you know how to spell the terms.

CHAPTER 12 QUIZ

1. Before mitosis, what process in the central dogma needs to occur for this process to occur? _____

2. [The answer to #1] occurs during _____ phase of interphase.

3. The enzyme that produces daughter strands of DNA by placing complementary nucleotides along each parental strand is called _____.

4. Why does this need to occur before mitosis? _____

    _____

5. A skein of DNA and proteins is called a _____.

6. Chromosomes are lined up at the spindle equator during

    _____.

7. DNA coils up into chromosomes, the spindle forms, and the nuclear envelope breaks up during _____.

8. Plant cytokinesis is accomplished through the formation of a

    _____ at the spindle equator.

9. Sister chromatids (one-copy chromosomes) migrate to opposite poles of the cell during _____ of mitosis.

10. When the spindle disappears, the chromosomes unravel, and the nuclear envelope reforms around each nucleus, the cell is in what phase of mitosis?

    _____.

CHAPTER 13

MEIOSIS

OBJECTIVES

1. Know why meiosis is necessary in making gametes or sex cells instead of mitosis.

2. Understand the concept of ploidy and what haploid and diploid means.

3. Understand what homologous chromosomes are.

4. Know what a human karyotype is. Be able to identify homologous chromosomes or sister chromatids on the karyotype.

5. Know where meiosis occurs in plants and animals.

6. Be able to describe what's happening in each phase of meiosis and why? In describing meiosis, be able to use any boldface terminology that is mentioned in the process.

7. Wherever meiosis differs from mitosis, be able to explain the reason for the differences.

8. Know what is meant by reduction division and when it occurs during meiosis.

 Thoroughly study the above objectives before you take the chapter quiz. Be sure you know how to spell the terms.

CHAPTER 13 QUIZ

1. Homologous chromosomes separate during _____.
    a. Anaphase of mitosis
    b. Anaphase I
    c. Anaphase II

2. The reduction division occurs during _____.
    a. Mitosis
    b. Meiosis I
    c. Meiosis II

3. Sister chromatids separate during _____.
    a. Anaphase I
    b. Anaphase II

4. Pairs of chromosomes that resemble each other in size, shape, and the genes they carry are called _____.

5. Crossing over occurs during _____.

6. What does crossing over accomplish in terms of offspring?

    _____

7. What is the big difference between metaphase of mitosis and metaphase I of meiosis? _____

    _____

8. Reduction division is when the cell changes in ploidy from

    _____ to _____.

9. Where does meiosis occur in animals and humans?

    In males? _____

    In females? _____

10. What does it produce in animals and humans?

    _____

THE BASICS *of* MENDELIAN GENETICS

OBJECTIVES

1. Know some basic historical background of Gregor Mendel.

2. Understand the meaning of the following terms: parental, F1, and F2 generations.

3. Be able to define alleles, homozygous (purebred), heterozygous (hybrid), genotype, phenotype, dominant, recessive, the Law of Segregation, and the Law of Independent Assortment.

4. Understand the relationship between the terms and phrases in each of the following bullet points:

    • Diploid, two letter genotype, and homologous pair of chromosomes.

    • Haploid, single letter gamete, and one chromosome from a homologous pair.

    • Given the genotypes of both parents, be able to symbolically figure out the gametes and the possible genotypes of the offspring using a Punnett Square. Also know how to figure out the genotypic and phenotypic ratios of the cross (this includes parental, monohybrid, dihybrid, and test crosses).

    • Given the genotypes of both parents be able to cross parents that exhibit codominance or incomplete dominance. Be able to figure out the offspring's genotypes and phenotypes (along with their ratios). Also understand both concepts.

    • Know the meaning of epistasis or polygenic inheritance.

 Thoroughly study the above objectives before you take the chapter quiz. Be sure you know how to spell the terms.

CHAPTER 14 QUIZ

1. Different versions of the same gene are called _____.

2. When a cell has two complete sets of genetic information it is said to be

   _____.

3. When a cell has one complete set of genetic information it is said to be

   _____.

4. The combination of alleles for a given gene is the organism's

   _____.

5. The actual physical appearance of the organism is _____.

Pea Traits
Y = yellow seeds (dominant)
y = green seeds (recessive)
R = round seeds (dominant)
r = wrinkled seeds (recessive)

6. Using a Punnett Square do the following monohybrid cross: F1: Yy x Yy.
   (First determine the possible gametes and place them in the first column and
   row; then fill in the Punnett square.)

7. What is the percentage of yellow seeded offspring in the F2 generation?_____

8. How do you determine whether yellow-seeded offspring is YY or Yy?

   _____

9. Using a Punnett Square do the following dihybrid cross: F1: YyRr x YyRr. (First determine the possible gametes and place them in the first column and row; then fill in the Punnett square.)

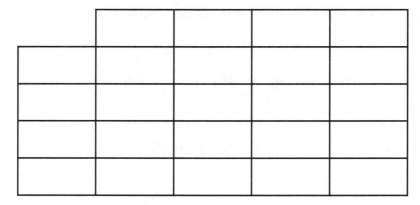

10. What percentage or proportion of offspring is green-round seeded? _____

11. What is the percentage or proportion of offspring is green-wrinkle seeded? _____

Hydra Traits (***Heterozygotes have six heads**)
F = Fire-breather (dominant)
f = non-fire breather (recessive)
*C = ten headed (incompletely dominant)
c = two headed

12. Using a Punnett Square do the following dihybrid cross: F1: FfCc x FfCc. (First determine the possible gametes and place them in the first column and row; then fill in the Punnett square.)

13. What is the phenotype of these F1 parents? _____

14. What percentage or proportion of F2 offspring can't breathe fire and has six heads? _____

15. What percentage or proportion of F2 offspring can breathe fire and has two heads? _____

 Study all the objectives for this unit. Make sure you know the correct answers for the quizzes. Understand the concepts and terms; don't just memorize them. Then take the Unit Exam.

UNIT 5 EXAM

1. Before mitosis, what process in the central dogma needs to occur for this process to occur? _____

2. [The answer to #1]y occurs during _____ phase of interphase.

3. The enzyme that produces daughter strands of DNA by placing complementary nucleotides along each parental strand is called

    _____.

4. Why does this need to occur before mitosis? _____

    _____

5. A skein of DNA and proteins is called a _____.

6. Chromosomes are lined up at the spindle equator during

    _____.

7. DNA coils up into chromosomes, the spindle forms, and the nuclear envelope breaks up during _____.

8. Plant cytokinesis is accomplished through the formation of a _____ at the spindle equator.

9. Animal cytokinesis is accomplished through a process called

    _____.

10. Sister chromatids (one-copy chromosomes) migrate to opposite poles of the cell during _____ of mitosis.

11. When the spindle disappears, the chromosomes unravel, and the nuclear envelope reforms around each nucleus, the cell is in what phase of mitosis? _____.

12. Homologous chromosomes separate during _____.
    a. Anaphase of mitosis
    b. Anaphase I
    c. Anaphase II

13. The reduction division occurs during _____.
    a. Mitosis
    b. Meiosis I
    c. Meiosis II

14. Sister chromatids separate during _____.
    a. Anaphase I
    b. Anaphase II

15. Meiosis forms spores in _____.

16. Which division in meiosis (I or II) is similar to mitosis? _____

17. Pairs of chromosomes that resemble each other in size, shape, and the genes they carry are called _____.

18. Crossing over occurs during _____.

19. What does crossing over accomplish in terms of offspring?

    _____

20. What is the big difference between metaphase of mitosis and metaphase I of meiosis? _____

21. Reduction division is when the cell changes in ploidy from

    _____ to _____ .

22. Where does meiosis occur in animals and humans?

    In males? _____

    In females? _____

23. What does meiosis produce in male animals (and humans)?

    _____

24. What does meiosis produce in female animals (and humans)?

    _____

25. Different versions of the same gene are called _____ .

26. When a cell has two complete sets of genetic information it is said to be

    _____ .

27. When a cell has one complete set of genetic information it is said to be

    _____ .

28. The combination of alleles for a given gene is the organism's

    _____ .

29. The actual physical appearance of the organism is _____ .

30. Pp is _____ because it has two

    different _____ for the same gene.

31. P symbolically represents the _____ allele

    for purple flowers because it overrides the effects of p, which is the

    _____ allele.

Pea Traits
Y = yellow seeds (dominant)
y = green seeds (recessive)
R = round seeds (dominant)
r = wrinkled seeds (recessive)

32. Using a Punnett Square do the following monohybrid cross: F1: Yy x Yy.
    (First determine the possible gametes and place them in the first column and
    row; then fill in the Punnett square.)

33. What is the percentage or proportion of yellow seeded offspring in the F2
    generation? _____

34. How do you determine whether yellow-seeded offspring is YY or Yy?
    _____

35. Using a Punnett Square do the following dihybrid cross: F1: YyRr x YyRr.
    (First determine the possible gametes and place them in the first column and
    row; then fill in the Punnett square.)

36. What percentage or proportion of offspring is green-round seeded? _____

37.   What is the percentage or proportion of offspring is green-wrinkle seeded? _____

Hydra Traits (***Heterozygotes have six heads**)
F = Fire-breather (dominant)
f = non-fire breather (recessive)
*C = ten headed (incompletely dominant)
c = two headed

38.   Using a Punnett Square do the following dihybrid cross: F1: FfCc x FfCc.

(First determine the possible gametes and place them in the first column and

row; then fill in the Punnett square.)

39.   What is the phenotype of these F1 parents? _____

40.   What proportion of F2 offspring can't breathe fire and has six heads? _____

41.   What proportion of F2 offspring can breathe fire and has two heads? _____

> ✳ Review the objectives of each chapter in Part I. Study the chapter quizzes and unit exams. Understand the material; don't just memorize it. Then take the Comprehensive Exam for Part I

COMPREHENSIVE EXAM FOR PART 1

1. The two subatomic particles contained in the nucleus of an atom are

    _____ and _____. What are their charges?

    (place the appropriate charge next to each name)

2. In a _____ covalent bond electrons are unevenly shared whereas

    in a _____ covalent bond electrons are evenly shared.

3. Draw a water molecule (H_2O) showing orbitals and shared electrons (atomic

    number of hydrogen: 1).

4. A move from pH 6 to pH 5 has made the solution _____ times more acidic.

    a. 2   b. 5   c. 10   d. 100

5. Name the four major biomolecule categories.

    a. _____

    b. _____

    c. _____

    d. _____

6. What are the 'TinkerToy rules' (how many bonds does it usually form with

    other atoms) for the following?

    a. Carbon _____

    b. Hydrogen _____

    c. Oxygen _____

    d. Nitrogen _____

    e. Phosphorus _____

    f. Sulfur _____

7.   Draw an amino acid doing a dehydration synthesis reaction with another amino acid to form a dipeptide. Label the peptide bond.

8.   Draw glucose.

9.   Who was the English scientist who coined the term cell? _____

10.   Who was the Dutchman who viewed microscopic life with a microscope of his own making? _____

11.   What are the three tenets of the Cell Theory?

   a.   _____

   b.   _____

   c.   _____

12.   Define diffusion: _____

_____

13.   Define osmosis: _____

_____

14. Movement of a substance across a membrane, through a protein gate but against a concentration gradient is called _____.

15. _____ are tiny organelles used in the construction of proteins.

16. The organelle that captures sunlight energy to make glucose out of carbon dioxide and water is the _____.

17. An organelle that contains digestive enzymes for the demolition of various biomolecules is the _____.

18. The law that states that matter cannot be created or destroyed but can be converted from one form to another is the

    _____.

19. Proteins that speed up chemical reactions millions of times faster are called

    _____.

20. Denaturation deforms or destroys the enzyme's _____.

21. CO_2 enters the leaf through openings in the epidermis called _____.

22. What are the two important products of the Light Dependent Reactions?

    a. _____

    b. _____

23. The cycle that produces glucose from CO_2 is called the
    _____ cycle. This cycle occurs in the
    _____ of the chloroplast.

24. Glycolysis occurs in the _____.

25. Phosphorylation (ADP + P → ATP) occurs when _____ ions flow through a channel protein/enzyme called _____.

26. In cellular respiration what important molecule from the air does all aerobic life need, that accepts electrons (and hydrogen) at the end of the Electron Transport System? _____

27. What is the grand total ATP yield from burning one molecule of glucose into $6CO_2$ and $6H_2O$? _____

28. Who were the two main discoverers (full names) of the structure of DNA?

    a. _____

    b. _____

29. What are the four different nitrogenous bases found in DNA?

    a. _____

    b. _____

    c. _____

    d. _____

30. If a DNA strand is T-A-C-G-C-G-C-T-T-G-A-T-T-T-A, what is the mRNA sequence? (Put a slash between codons)

    _____

31. What is the amino acid sequence? (Use the three letter abbreviations for the amino acids; refer to the following genetic code.) **Place genetic code table here**

    _____

    _____

32. What organism is the lac operon in? _____

33. What is the place on DNA to which RNA polymerase attaches at the beginning of transcription? _____

34. What protein attaches to the operator to prevent certain genes from being transcribed in the lac operon?_____

35. Enzymes used to cut DNA at specific sequences are called

    _____ enzymes.

36. The enzyme used to splice DNA fragments together is called

    _____.

37. List the seven basic steps in recombinant DNA technology.

    a. _____

    b. _____

    c. _____

    d. _____

    e. _____

    f. _____

    g. _____

38. Before mitosis, what process in the central dogma needs to occur for this

    process to occur? _____

39. Chromosomes are lined up at the spindle equator during

    _____ of mitosis.

40. When the spindle disappears, the chromosomes unravel, and the nuclear

    envelope reforms around each nucleus, the cell is in what phase of mitosis?

    _____.

41. Homologous chromosomes separate during _____.

    a. Anaphase of mitosis

    b. Anaphase I

    c. Anaphase II

42. Pairs of chromosomes that resemble each other in size, shape, and the genes

    they carry are called _____.

43. During meiosis reduction division is when the cell changes in ploidy from

    _____ to _____ .

44. During meiosis sister chromatids separate during _____ .

    a. Anaphase I
    b. Anaphase II

45. The combination of alleles for a given gene is the organism's

    _____ .

46. The actual physical appearance of the organism is _____ .

    Hydra Traits (***Heterozygotes have six heads**)
    F = Fire-breather (dominant)
    f = non-fire breather (recessive)
    *C = ten headed (incompletely dominant)
    c = two headed

47. Using a Punnett Square do the following dihybrid cross: F1: FfCc x FfCc.
    (First determine the possible gametes and place them in the first column and
    row; then fill in the Punnett square.)

48. What percentage or proportion of F2 offspring can't breathe fire and has six
    heads? _____

49. What percentage or proportion of F2 offspring can breathe fire and has two
    heads? _____

PART 2

DIVERSITY OF LIFE

CLASSIFYING LIFE

OBJECTIVES

1. Know the main figures and their key works that contributed to the science of taxonomy throughout world history.

2. Know what determines how a taxonomist classifies animals or plants or anything.

3. Know the major difference in impetus for classification pre and post Darwin.

4. Know and understand the current levels of biological classification initially devised by Linnaeus. Be able to describe the different levels using weevils.

5. Understand the 'why' and rules of scientific naming.

6. Know the definition of species and subspecies.

7. Be able to explain the different interpretations of the diversity of life: the Linnaean Lawn, the Evolutionary Tree, and the Creationist Orchard.

8. From a creationist perspective understand and be conversant with the bold-faced terms in the "Modern Taxonomy through Evolutionary Eyes" section. Be able to see the internal logic of their worldview while also seeing why their premise is false.

 Thoroughly study the above objectives before you take the chapter quiz. Be sure you know how to spell the terms.

CHAPTER 15 QUIZ

1. One of the first taxonomists of the fourth century B.C. was _____ .

2. Different classification schemes result from differences of opinion on what _____ are the most important to compare or contrast.

3. A Swedish naturalist named _____

    was the father of modern taxonomy. He proposed the

    _____ system of naming that is still

    used today.

4. What are the seven ranks (taxa) in the classification hierarchy below domain
    that Linnaeus developed but was added to? Go from general to specific.

    a. Domain

    b. _____

    c. _____

    d. _____

    e. _____

    f. _____

    g. _____

    h. _____

5. Similar families are grouped into a single _____ .

6. A class is split into several _____ .

7. The binomial of the American toad is "bufo americanus." Rewrite it

    correctly: _____

    What is its genus name? _____

    Species name? _____

    Specific epithet? _____

8. Draw a Creationist Orchard and circle one baramin.

9. From an evolutionary perspective, butterfly wings and bat wings would be considered _____ structures because they didn't evolve from the same feature in their common ancestor.

10. A baramin is _____.
    a. Monophyletic
    b. Polyphyletic
    c. Paraphyletic

11. From an evolutionary perspective, front flippers in dolphins and human arms would be considered _____ structures because they did evolve from the same feature in their common ancestor.

12. From an evolutionary perspective, the evolution of a totally new anatomical feature (a derived character) is considered a(n) _____.

13. If two or more clades are lumped into one group because they share a common feature but the grouping excludes the common ancestor and other members that would unite them into a single clade, it is termed

    _____.

14. Creationists object to evolution when it involves the _____.
    a. Minor modification of a plesiomorphy
    b. Addition of an apomorphy.

THE VIRUSES AND PROKARYOTES

OBJECTIVES

1. Know the parts of a virus, how it infects host cells, and multiples itself within.

2. Know the parts of a generalized prokaryotic cell (bacterial cell).

3. Know the basic shapes and groupings of bacteria.

4. Qualitatively know the proportion of good to bad bacteria and be able to use terms like decomposers, cyanobacteria, pathogenic bacteria in describing both the good and bad roles they play in nature.

5. Know the major groups of kingdom Archaea and know what special abilities each has.

 Thoroughly study the above objectives before you take the chapter quiz. Be sure you know how to spell the terms.

CHAPTER 16 QUIZ

1. The viral _____ is a protein container for

    _____ or _____.

2. True or false? Viruses have their own metabolism apart from the host cells they infect.

3. True or false? Viruses only infect animals and humans.

4. The two major groups of prokaryotes are the _____

    and the _____.

5. Bacterial cell walls are made of a polysaccharide called

    _____

6. Cytoplasmic tunnels that temporarily connect bacterial cells and allow for the transfer of genetic information are called _____.

7. A chain of rod-shaped bacteria hooked end to end are termed

    _____.

8. Besides the circular chromosome, bacteria often contain smaller hoops of DNA called _____.

9. Most species of bacteria _____
    a. are disease-causing (pathogenic).
    b. do not cause disease but aren't beneficial to the environment.
    c. perform many beneficial ecological functions.

10. Which one of the following Archaean groups is not an extremophile?
    a. Halophiles
    b. Methanogens
    c. Acidophiles
    d. Thermophiles

CHAPTER 17

 ALGAE

PLANT-LIKE PROTISTS

OBJECTIVES

1. Know why protists don't really form a unified group.

2. Know the major groups of algae (Euglenoids, Dinoflagellates, Diatoms, Brown Algae, Red Algae, and Green Algae), their notable or unique characteristics (including specific examples in each group), and their basic natural history.

 Thoroughly study the above objectives before you take the chapter quiz. Be sure you know how to spell the terms.

CHAPTER 17 QUIZ

1. A complex arrangement of contractile proteins beneath the cell membrane of euglenoids that enable them to change shape is called a _____.

2. Some photosynthetic euglenoids have a _____ that is light sensitive and enables them to determine the direction of the light and swim towards it.

3. Free-living dinoflagellates have two flagella. One is situated in a _____ groove. The other is in a _____ groove.

4. Red tide is caused by a population explosion of certain species of _____.
   a. Dinoflagellates
   b. Diatoms
   c. Red algae

5. Which marine algal group is the most important photosynthesizer of the oceans?
   _____

6. The toxic chemicals that make red tide dangerous to certain sea life are _____.

7. What lives in the tissues of corals that enable them to live in such nutrient-poor water? _____
   What do these microscopic tenants produce? _____
   How do they produce it? _____

8. Certain kinds of _____ are able to undergo bioluminescence.

9. The beautiful cell walls of diatoms are composed of _____ compounds.

10. All photosynthetic (autotrophic) protists are termed _____.

11. _____ is a multipurpose product extracted from certain types of brown algae.

12. What are the technical names of these seaweed groups?

    a. Brown Algae—_____

    b. Red Algae -_____

    c. Green Algae—_____

13. Their photosynthetic _____ serve as the basis of their classification.

14. Brown algae often have four major organs that compose their body:

    a. The _____ which is used for anchoring the algae to the sea floor.

    b. The _____ which acts a flexible stem or stalk.

    c. The _____ which is analogous to a leaf and serves as the primary area of photosynthesis.

    d. The _____ which is gas filled and grants buoyancy to some underwater seaweeds.

15. _____ is a polysaccharide extracted from certain types of red algae and is used as a gel-like material for bacteria to grow on in Petri dishes.

 Study all the objectives for this unit. Make sure you know the correct answers for the quizzes. Understand the concepts and terms; don't just memorize them. Then take the Unit Exam.

UNIT 6 EXAM

1. One of the first taxonomists of the fourth century B.C. was _____ .

2. Different classification schemes result from differences of opinion on what _____ are the most important to compare or contrast.

3. A Swedish naturalist named _____ was the father of modern taxonomy. He proposed the _____ system of naming that is still used today.

4. What are the seven ranks (taxa) in the classification hierarchy below domain that Linnaeus developed but was added to? Go from general to specific.

    a. Domain

    b. _____

    c. _____

    d. _____

    e. _____

    f. _____

    g. _____

    h. _____

5. Similar families are grouped into a single _____ .

6. A class is split into several _____ .

7. The binomial of the American toad is bufo americanus. Rewrite it correctly.

    _____

    What is its genus name? _____

    Species name? _____

    Specific epithet? _____

8.   Draw a Creationist Orchard and circle one baramin.

9.   Draw an Evolutionary Tree.

10. Draw a Linnaean Lawn (what does each vertical line represent?)

11. Whose writing was most influential in causing a paradigm shift from a
     Linnaean Lawn view of life to an Evolutionary Tree view of life?

     _____

12. From an evolutionary perspective, butterfly wings and bat wings would be
     considered _____ structures because they didn't
     evolve from the same feature in their common ancestor.

13. A baramin is _____.

    a. Monophyletic
    b. Polyphyletic
    c. Paraphyletic

14. From an evolutionary perspective, front flippers in dolphins and human arms would be considered _____ structures because they did evolve from the same feature in their common ancestor.

15. From an evolutionary perspective, the evolution of a totally new anatomical feature (a derived character) is considered a(n) _____.

16. If two or more clades are lumped into one group because they share a common feature but the grouping excludes the common ancestor and other members that would unite them into a single clade, it is termed _____ .

17. Creationists object to evolution when it involves the _____.

    a. Minor modification of a plesiomorphy
    b. Addition of an apomorphy.

18. The viral _____ is a protein container for _____ or _____ .

19. True or false? Viruses have their own metabolism apart from the host cells they infect.

20. True or false? Viruses only infect animals and humans.

21. The two major groups of prokaryotes are the _____ and the _____ .

22. Bacterial cell walls are made of a polysaccharide called _____ .

23. Cytoplasmic tunnels that temporarily connect bacterial cells and allow for the transfer of genetic information are called _____ .

24. A chain of rod-shaped bacteria hooked end to end are called

_____.

25. Spherical bacteria clustered in pairs are called _____.

26. Besides the circular chromosome, bacteria often contain smaller hoops of DNA called _____.

27. Most species of bacteria...

    a. are disease-causing (pathogenic).
    b. do not cause disease but aren't beneficial to the environment.
    c. perform many beneficial ecological functions.

28. Which one of the following Archaean groups is not an extremophile?

    a. Halophiles
    b. Methanogens
    c. Acidophiles
    d. Thermophiles

29. Halophiles are _____ loving prokaryotes.

30. True or false? No thermophiles can tolerate temperatures over the boiling point of water.

31. A complex arrangement of contractile proteins beneath the cell membrane of euglenoids that enable them to change shape is called a

_____.

32. Some photosynthetic euglenoids have a _____ that is light sensitive and enables them to determine the direction of the light and swim towards it.

33. Free-living dinoflagellates have two flagella. One is situated in a

_____ groove. The other is in a

_____ groove.

34. Red tide is caused by a population explosion of certain species of _____.

    a. Dinoflagellates
    b. Diatoms
    c. Red algae

35. Which marine algal group is the most important photosynthesizer of the oceans? _____.

36. The toxic chemicals that make red tide dangerous to certain sea life are

    _____.

37. Diatomaceous earth is composed of massive deposits of diatom

    _____.

38. What lives in the tissues of corals that enable them to live in such nutrient poor water? _____

39. What do [the answer to #39] produce? _____
    And how do they produce it? _____

40. Certain kinds of _____ are able to undergo bioluminescence.

41. The beautiful cell walls of diatoms are composed of _____ compounds.

42. All photosynthetic (autotrophic) protists are termed _____.

43. _____ is a multipurpose product extracted from certain types of brown algae.

44. What are the technical names of these seaweed groups?

    a. Brown Algae: _____

    a. Red Algae: _____

    b. Green Algae: _____

45. Their photosynthetic _____ serve as the basis of their classification.

46. Brown algae often have four major organs that compose their body.

    a. The _____ which is used for anchoring the algae to the sea floor.

    b. The _____ which acts a flexible stem or stalk.

    c. The _____ which is analogous to a leaf and serves as the primary area of photosynthesis.

    d. The _____ which is a gas filled and grants buoyancy to some underwater seaweeds.

47. Which group of algae is thought to be the direct ancestors of the plant kingdom?

    _____

48. What trait in this group leads them to this conclusion? _____

49. _____ is a polysaccharide extracted from certain types of red algae and is used as a gel-like material for bacteria to grow on in Petri dishes.

ANIMAL-LIKE AND FUNGAL-LIKE PROTISTS

OBJECTIVE

Know the major groups of protozoa (Flagellates, Amebas and relatives, and Ciliates) and fungal-like protists (Plasmodial Slime Molds, Cellular Slime Molds, and Water Molds), their notable or unique characteristics (including specific examples in each group), and their basic natural history.

 Thoroughly study the above objectives before you take the chapter quiz. Be sure you know how to spell the terms.

CHAPTER 18 QUIZ

1. The flagellates share a locomotion device called a device called a
    _____.

2. Shelled amebas that produce a calcium carbonate test (shell) are called
    _____.

3. *Giardia*, *Trichonympha*, and *Trypanosoma* are all examples of a disease-causing _____

4. Shelled amebas that produce a test composed of glass compounds are called
    _____.

5. White Cliffs of Dover are partly composed of the shells of which protozoan
    group? _____

6. Protozoans that get around with and obtain food with cilia are classified in
    the group called _____.

7. The common feature of all amebas is the _____
    which is an extension of the cell used for locomotion and feeding.

8. All single-celled, non-photosynthetic (heterotrophic) protists resembling little
    animals are called _____.

9. Many freshwater protozoa have an osmotic problem because they live in a
    hypotonic environment. What organelle do they possess that helps them cope
    with the constant influx of water? _____

10. Many ciliates have a depression on their cell surface where they channel food to
    be phagocytosed. This is called the _____.

11. A plasmodial slime mold is a gigantic multinucleate blob that resembles fungi by
    producing _____ which produce spores.

12. The 'slug' in cellular slime molds differs with the plasmodium in that it is composed of many _____ moving together.

13. Water molds differ from Fungi in two significant ways.

   a. They have a cell wall made of _____ rather than chitin.

   b. They are _____ (ploidy) for most of their life cycle.

14. Name the water mold that had a great historical impact in Ireland.

   _____

15. What was the historical impact? In other words, what did the water mold do that had a huge impact on the United States? _____

   _____

   _____

   _____

KINGDOM FUNGI

OBJECTIVES

1. Know the characteristics of Kingdom Fungi.

2. Be able to describe the good deeds and dirty deeds of fungi.

3. Know the major groups of Fungi (the Zygomycetes, the Ascomycetes, and the Basidiomycetes), their unique characteristics (including specific notable examples in each group), and their basic natural history.

4. Know what two types of organisms form lichens. Be able to describe how they benefit from each other in their mutualism. Also know the three major growth forms of lichen.

5. Be able to describe the mutualism of mycorrhizae with vascular plant roots.

 Thoroughly study the above objectives before you take the chapter quiz. Be sure you know how to spell the terms.

CHAPTER 19 QUIZ

1. List six characteristics of Fungi other than eukaryotic, heterotrophic, and multicellular.

    a. _____

    b. _____

    c. _____

    d. _____

    e. _____

    f. _____

2. Fungi obtain nutrients through a process called _____ digestion. This occurs when the hyphae exocytose _____ releasing digestive enzymes onto the surrounding organic material.

3. Name two destructive activities of fungi.

    a. _____

    b. _____

4. Name three beneficial activities of fungi.

    a. _____

    b. _____

    c. _____

5. The zygomycete fungi reproduce asexually from spores that have been released from knob-like spore containers called _____.

6. In the black bread mold, tough spore containers called _____ are formed from the sexual union of two different mating strains.

7. Zygomycetes have hyphae with different job-descriptions and special names. The root-like _____ penetrate the substrate and absorb nutrients.

8. Ascomycete fungi reproduce asexually by spores called

    _____ that form pop-it bead-like chains.

9. Ascomycete fungi, during the sexual phase form fruiting bodies called

    _____. The concave (usually) spore-

    producing surface called the *hymenium* is formed by one layer of densely

    packed parallel _____ each containing

    eight _____.

10. An atypical ascomycete is _____ and is essential in

    the brewing and baking industry.

11. The shelf fungi, mushrooms, puffballs, earthstars, and coral fungi are all

    examples of _____.

12. In mushrooms, the hymenium is the surface of the _____

    and is composed of parallel-arranged basidia. Each one forms four

    _____ which eventually get placed on

    the outside surface until they drop off.

13. Lichens are formed by a mutualistic relationship between

    _____

    and _____.

14. The growth form of lichen that is bushy and branching is called:

    a. Fruticose   b. Foliose   c. Crustose

15. Fungi called _____ form a

    mutualistic relationship with vascular plant roots. The fungi benefits from

    the _____ of the plant and the plant benefits

    because the fungi enhances _____ and

    _____ absorption for the plant.

KINGDOM ANIMALIA
A SHORT INTRODUCTION

OBJECTIVES

1. Know the characteristics of Kingdom Animalia.

2. Be able to name and describe the types three of symmetry and the lack thereof. Be able to give one or two examples of each.

3. Know the vertebrate/invertebrate distinction and which one spans the vast majority of animals. Know the phylum that includes vertebrates.

 Thoroughly study the above objectives before you take the chapter quiz. Be sure you know how to spell the terms.

CHAPTER 20 QUIZ

1. List five general characteristics of all animals.

    a. _____

    b. _____

    c. _____

    d. _____

    e. _____

2. What type of tissue grants animals the ability to move? _____

3. In what type of symmetry can an animal be divided into only two mirror image halves by only one plane?_____

4. What is the most common symmetry of animals? _____

5. Name two animal groups that show [answer to #3] symmetry.

    a. _____

    b. _____

6. If an animal is divided into similar halves by more than two planes running through the central axis of an animal it has _____ symmetry.

7. Name two animals that show [answer to #6] symmetry.

    a. _____

    b. _____

8. Name one animal that is asymmetrical. _____.

9. Between invertebrates and vertebrates, which spans the most phyla?

    _____

10. Phylum _____ is composed almost entirely of vertebrates.

 Study all the objectives for this unit. Make sure you know the correct answers for the quizzes. Understand the concepts and terms; don't just memorize them. Then take the Unit Exam.

UNIT 7 EXAM

1. The flagellates share a locomotion device called a _____.

2. Shelled amebas that produce a calcium carbonate test (shell) are called _____.

3. *Giardia*, *Trichonympha*, and *Trypanosoma* are all examples of a disease-causing _____.

4. Shelled amebas that produce a test composed of glass compounds are called _____.

5. The White Cliffs of Dover are partly composed of the shells of which protozoan group? _____

6. Protozoans that get around with and obtain food with cilia are classified in the group called _____.

7. The common feature of all amebas is the _____ which is an extension of the cell used for locomotion and feeding.

8. All single-celled, non-photosynthetic (heterotrophic) protists resembling little animals are called _____.

9. Many freshwater protozoa have an osmotic problem because they live in a hypotonic environment. What organelle do they possess that helps them cope with the constant influx of water? _____

10. Many ciliates have a depression on their cell surface where they channel food to be phagocytosed. This is called the _____.

11. A plasmodial slime mold is a gigantic multinucleate blob that resembles fungi by producing _____ , which produce spores.

12. The 'slug' in cellular slime molds differs with the plasmodium in that it is composed of many _____ moving together.

13. Water molds differ from Fungi in two significant ways:

    a. They have a cell wall made of _____ rather than chitin.

    b. They are _____ (ploidy) for most of their life cycle.

14. Name the water mold that had a great historical impact in Ireland.

    _____

15. What was the historical impact? In other words, what did the water mold do that had a huge impact on the United States? _____

    _____

    _____

16. List six characteristics of Fungi other than eukaryotic, heterotrophic, and multicellular.

    a. _____

    b. _____

    c. _____

    d. _____

    e. _____

    f. _____

17. Fungi obtain nutrients through a process called _____ digestion. This occurs when the hyphae exocytose_____ releasing digestive enzymes onto the surrounding organic material.

18. Name two destructive activities of fungi.

    a. _____

    b. _____

19. Name three beneficial activities of fungi.

    a. _____

    b. _____

    c. _____

20. The zygomycete fungi reproduce asexually from spores that have been released from knob-like spore containers called _____.

21. In black bread mold, tough spore containers called _____ are formed from the sexual union of two different mating strains.

22. Zygomycetes have hyphae with different job-descriptions and special names. The root-like _____ penetrate the substrate and absorb nutrients.

23. Ascomycete fungi reproduce asexually by spores called _____ that form pop-it bead-like chains.

24. Ascomycete fungi, during the sexual phase form fruiting bodies called _____. The concave (usually) spore-producing surface called the *hymenium* is formed by one layer of densely packed parallel _____ each containing eight _____.

25. An atypical ascomycete is _____ and is essential in the brewing and baking industry.

26. The shelf fungi, mushrooms, puffballs, earthstars, and coral fungi are all examples of _____.

27. In mushrooms, the hymenium is the surface of the _____ and is composed of parallel-arranged basidia. Each one forms four _____ which eventually get placed on the outside surface until they drop off.

28. Lichens are formed by a mutualistic relationship between

    _____

    and _____.

29. The growth form of lichen that is bushy and branching is called:

    a. Fruticose
    b. Foliose
    c. Crustose

30. Fungi called _____ form a
    mutualistic relationship with vascular plant roots. The fungi benefits from
    the _____ of the plant and the plant benefits
    because the fungi enhances _____ and
    _____ absorption for the plant.

31. List five general characteristics of all animals.

    a. _____

    b. _____

    c. _____

    d. _____

    e. _____

32. What type of tissue grants animals the ability to move? _____
    _____

33. What is the symmetry where the animal can only be divided into two mirror
    image halves by only one plane? _____

34. What is the most common symmetry of animals? _____

35. Name two animal groups that show [answer to #34] symmetry.

    a. _____

    b. _____

36. If an animal is divided into similar halves by more than two planes running through the central axis of an animal it has _____ symmetry.

37. Name two animals that show [answer to #36] symmetry.

    a. _____

    b. _____

38. Name one animal that is asymmetrical. _____

39. Between invertebrates and vertebrates, which spans the most phyla?

    _____

40. Phylum _____ is almost entirely composed of vertebrates.

PHYLUM PORIFERA
THE SPONGES

OBJECTIVES

1. Know the basic anatomy and natural history (habitat, feeding, reproduction, etc.) of Phylum Porifera.

2. Be able to identify the three major body forms of sponges.

3. Be able to trace with arrows the water flow through a syconoid sponge.

 Thoroughly study the above objectives before you take the chapter quiz. Be sure you know how to spell the terms.

CHAPTER 21 QUIZ

1. Sponges are _____-feeders because they strain out microscopic plankton from the water that circulates through them.

2. Sponge skeletons are composed of beautiful siliceous or calcareous _____ that provide rigidity.

3. The specialized cells in a sponge that generate the water current and capture and phagocytose the microscopic plankton are called _____ cells.

4. What is the protein that serves as a flexible skeleton for sponges?

   _____

5. What canals are lined with collar cells in syconoid sponges?

   _____

6. Asexual reproduction in sponges occurs through budding and by the production of tiny tough capsules containing sponge cells called _____ that can survive adverse environmental conditions.

7. Draw a simple body outline of a syconoid sponge (using dashes to show the pores or prosopyles). Label the incurrent canal, radial canal, spongocoel, and osculum. Use an arrow to show the pattern of water flow through the sponge.

8. In the more complicated leuconoid sponge, what is lined with collar cells?

   _____

9.   What important ecological service do sponges perform as they filter feed?

_____

10. In sexual reproduction of most sponges, the sperm and egg cells are produced in:

    a. the same sponge.

    b. different male and female sponges.

PHYLUM CNIDARIA

JELLYFISH, SEA ANEMONES, CORAL, ETC.

OBJECTIVES

1. Know the basic anatomy of Phylum Cnidaria.

2. Know the structure and function of cnidocytes and their nematocysts within.

3. Know the three classes of Cnidaria and some examples of each. Also know which body form these classes usually have.

4. Be able to describe the life cycle of a jellyfish.

 Thoroughly study the above objectives before you take the chapter quiz. Be sure you know how to spell the terms.

CHAPTER 22 QUIZ

1. The hallmark characteristic of phylum Cnidaria are the possession of cells called cnidocytes which contain stinging organelles called _____ .

2. Cnidocytes are mostly concentrated in bands in the epidermis on which body part?
   a. Stalk
   b. Pedal disk
   c. Tentacles
   d. Mouth

3. True or false? All nematocysts are designed to sting.

4. Finger-like projections of the body wall surround the mouth and are called

   _____ .

5. Once triggered _____ flows into the capsule from the cytoplasm of the cnidocyte causing the nematocyst to be discharged. Then _____ flows out into the prey through the tube.

6. There are two general body forms of Cnidaria: the _____ and the _____ .

7. Hydra, coral, hydroid colonies, and sea anemones exhibit the _____ form while jellyfish exhibit the _____ form.

8. The digestive system of Cnidarians is composed mostly of the mouth and the _____ cavity. Solid waste must be excreted out of the _____ .

9. Generally there are two cell layers that comprise the body wall: the _____ and the _____ .

10. Nutrients are absorbed by which cell layer? _____

11. Name two prey items of larger sea anemones.

    a. _____

    b. _____

12. Name two very different ways coral polyps can feed themselves.

    a. _____

    b. _____

13. The Portuguese Man-of-war is a:

    a. colony of polyps.

    b. jellyfish.

14. Sperm and eggs from the gonads are released out of the _____
    of separate male and female jellyfish. Fertilization happens in the open sea water
    and the zygote grows into a small ciliated larva called a _____.

15. A thin to thick non-cellular layer is sandwiched between the epidermis and
    gastrodermis and is called the _____.

CHAPTER 23

THE WORMS

1. Know the distinguishing characteristics of these three major phyla of worms.

2. Be able to describe the basic natural history of each representative worm and any unique anatomy it possesses. Also, know the phylum and class (if given) that each belongs in and why.

 Thoroughly study the above objectives before you take the chapter quiz. Be sure you know how to spell the terms.

CHAPTER 23 QUIZ

1. Phylum _____ are the flatworms because they
    are all dorsoventrally flattened.

2. Name the three classes of flatworms (common name of the class is fine).

    a. _____

    b. _____

    c. _____

3. The tapeworms don't need a digestive tract because _____

    _____

4. Which two classes of flatworms have an incomplete digestive tract?

    a. _____

    b. _____

5. Which class of flatworm is parasitic and has a mollusk for a primary host and a
    vertebrate for a final host? _____

6. The tapeworms have segments called _____
    that detach and leave the host with the feces when they mature and are
    loaded with eggs.

7. Tapeworms anchor themselves to the gut lining using hooks and or suckers
    mounted on the head-like _____.

8. Planaria are known, after being cut in pieces, for each piece to
    _____ the missing parts.

9. The planaria's mouth is located on the end of a hose-like
    _____ which is positioned in the
    middle of the underside. Incoming food is brought into its
    _____ cavity.

10. Roundworms:

    a. have tapered ends.

    b. have a complete digestive system.

    c. are round in cross section.

    d. all the above

    e. only a and b

    f. only a and c

    g. only b and c

11. Roundworms belong to Phylum _____.

12. How does their digestive tract differ from Phylum Platyhelminthes?

    _____

13. Many filarial worms cause massive swelling that is due to the blockage of _____ coming back from the extremities. The swelling is also aggravated by the victim's immune response called _____. This disfiguring disease is called _____.

14. Filial worm larvae are injected into human hosts by a _____ which is the intermediate host.

15. The segmented worms belong to Phylum _____.

16. List three major classes of segmented worms.

    a. _____

    b. _____

    c. _____

17. True or false? Earthworms are the only kind of oligochaetes.

18. Name three ways earthworms benefit the soil.

     a. _____

     b. _____

     c. _____

19. True or false? All leeches suck blood or body fluids out of their prey.

20. What class of segmented worms is mostly found in marine (ocean water) environments? _____

 Study all the objectives for this unit. Make sure you know the correct answers for the quizzes. Understand the concepts and terms; don't just memorize them. Then take the Unit Exam.

UNIT 8 EXAM

1. Sponges are _____-feeders because they strain out microscopic plankton from the water that circulates through them.

2. Sponge skeletons are composed of beautiful siliceous or calcareous _____ that provide rigidity.

3. The specialized cells in a sponge that generate the water current, capture, and phagocytose the microscopic plankton are called _____ cells.

4. What is the protein that serves as a flexible skeleton for sponges?

    _____

5. What canals are lined with collar cells in syconoid sponges?

    _____

6. Asexual reproduction in sponges occurs through budding and by the production of tiny tough capsules containing sponge cells called _____ that can survive adverse environmental conditions.

7. Draw a simple body outline of a syconoid sponge (using dashes to show the pores or prosopyles). Label the incurrent canal, radial canal, spongocoel, and osculum. Use an arrow to show the pattern of water flow through the sponge.

8. In the more complicated leuconoid sponge, what is lined with collar cells?

    _____

9. What important ecological service do sponges perform as they filter feed?

    _____

10. In sexual reproduction of most sponges, the sperm and egg cells are produced in:

    a. the same sponge.
    b. different male and female sponges.

11. The hallmark characteristic of phylum Cnidaria are the possession of cells called cnidocytes which contain stinging organelles called _____ .

12. Cnidocytes are mostly concentrated in bands in the epidermis on which body part?

    a. Stalk   b. Pedal disk   c. Tentacles   d. Mouth

13. True or false? All nematocysts are designed to sting. _____

14. Finger-like projections of the body wall surround the mouth and are called

    _____.

15. Once triggered _____ flows into the capsule from the cytoplasm of the cnidocyte causing the nematocyst to be discharged. Then _____ flows out into the prey through the tube.

16. There are two general body forms of Cnidaria:

    the _____ and the _____ .

17. Hydra, coral, hydroid colonies, and sea anemones exhibit the _____ form while jellyfish exhibit the _____ form.

18. The digestive system of Cnidarians is composed mostly of the mouth and the _____ cavity. Solid waste must be excreted out of the _____ .

19. Generally there are two cell layers that comprise the body wall:

    the _____ and the _____.

20. Nutrients are absorbed by which cell layer? _____

21. Name two prey items of larger sea anemones.

    a. _____

    b. _____

22. Name two very different ways coral polyps can feed themselves.

    a. _____

    b. _____

23. The Portuguese Man-of-war is a:

    a. colony of polyps.
    b. jellyfish.

24. Sperm and eggs from the gonads are released out of the

    _____ of separate male and female

    jellyfish. Fertilization happens in the open sea water and the zygote grows

    into a small ciliated larva called a _____.

25. A thin to thick non-cellular layer is sandwiched between the epidermis and

    gastrodermis and is called the _____.

26. Phylum _____ are the flatworms

    because they are all dorsoventrally flattened.

27. Name the three classes of flatworms (common name of the class is fine).

    a. _____

    b. _____

    c. _____

28. The tapeworms don't need a digestive tract because _____

_____.

29. Which two classes of flatworms have an incomplete digestive tract?

    a. _____

    b. _____

30. Which class of flatworm is parasitic and has a mollusk for a primary host and a vertebrate for a final host? _____

31. The tapeworms have segments called _____ that detach and leave the host with the feces when they mature and are loaded with eggs.

32. True or false? These tapeworm segments only have male or female gonads; never both.

33. Tapeworms anchor themselves to the gut lining using hooks and or suckers mounted on the head-like _____.

34. Planaria are known, after being cut in pieces, for each piece to

_____ the missing parts.

35. The planaria's mouth is located on the end of a hose-like _____,
which is positioned in the middle of the underside. Incoming food is brought into its _____ cavity.

36. Roundworms:
    a. have tapered ends.
    b. have a complete digestive system.
    c. are round in cross section.
    d. all the above
    e. only a and b
    f. only a and c
    g. only b and c

37. Roundworms belong to Phylum _____.

38. How does their digestive tract differ from Phylum Platyhelminthes?

     _____

39. Many filarial worms cause massive swelling that is due to the blockage of

     _____ coming back from the extremities.

40. This swelling due to the blockage is also aggravated by the victim's immune

     response called _____.

41. [The answer to #40] is caused by filarial worms is called

     _____ .

42. Filial worm larvae are injected into human hosts by a

     _____ which is the intermediate host.

43. The segmented worms belong to Phylum _____.

44. List three major classes of segmented worms.

     a. _____

     b. _____

     c. _____

45. True or false? Terrestrial earthworms are the only kind of oligochaetes.

46. True or false? Among annelids, polychaetes are the only group that has bristles.

47. Name three ways earthworms benefit the soil.

     a. _____

     b. _____

     c. _____

48. True or false? All leeches suck blood or body fluids out of their prey.

49. Which of the following annelid classes don't have bristles?

    a. Oligochaetes
    b. Polychaetes
    c. Hirudinea

50. What class of segmented worms is mostly found in marine (ocean water) environments? _____

PHYLUM MOLLUSCA

THE MOLLUSKS: CLAMS, OYSTERS, SNAILS, SLUGS, SQUIDS, ETC.

OBJECTIVES

1. Know the major characteristics of mollusks.

2. Know the distinguishing characteristics and basic natural history of the three major classes of mollusks. Be able to name some representative examples of each class and why they belong to it.

 Thoroughly study the above objectives before you take the chapter quiz. Be sure you know how to spell the terms.

CHAPTER 24 QUIZ

1. List six characteristics of mollusks (one is possessed by most but not all mollusks).

    a. _____

    b. _____

    c. _____

    d. _____

    e. _____

    f. _____

2. The _____ secretes the shell in mollusks.

3. Which class of mollusks are filter feeders? _____

4. The tongue-like rasping organ in many mollusks is the _____ .

5. Name three mollusks that don't have a shell of any kind.

    a. _____

    b. _____

    c. _____

6. In bivalves, what organ collects plankton on its surface and sweeps it toward the mouth with cilia? _____

7. In bivalves, what organ is the gateway of water into the mantle cavity?

    _____

8. What organ is the exit of water out of the bivalve? _____

9. By expanding and contracting their mantle, cephalopods accomplish at least two important things. They are:

    a. _____

    b. _____

10. Cephalopods have an _____ from which black fluid is expelled out the funnel to confuse and distract predators in an attempt to get away.

11. Name three types of cephalopods.

    a. _____

    b. _____

    c. _____

12. Name three types of bivalves.

    a. _____

    b. _____

    c. _____

13. Name three types of gastropods.

    a. _____

    b. _____

    c. _____

14. Slugs and land snails have two pair of tentacles. What do the upper ones have at their tips? _____

15. Slugs have a _____ which serves as an organ of respiration.

PHYLUM ARTHROPODA

THE ARTHROPODS: CRUSTACEANS, ARACHNIDS, INSECTS, ETC.

OBJECTIVES

1. Know the major characteristics of Arthropods.

2. Know the distinguishing characteristics and basic natural history of the following taxa:

   Trilobites, Diplopods, Chilopods, Crustaceans, Insects, and Arachnids (plus the different taxa within the Crustaceans, Insects, and Arachnids).

3. Be able to name the representative examples of each taxon and why they belong to it.

 Thoroughly study the above objectives before you take the chapter quiz. Be sure you know how to spell the terms.

CHAPTER 25 QUIZ

1. List four major characteristics of the arthropods.

    a. _____

    b. _____

    c. _____

    d. _____

2. Arthropod means _____.

3. In the molting process, the new cuticle is produced _____ the old cuticle.

    a. Underneath

    b. On the outside of

4. An extinct group of arthropods having a head, thorax, and pygidium is the

    _____.

5. Slow, graceful arthropods that feed on lichens, detritus, and some plants and
    have two pairs of legs per segment (on most segments) are the

    _____ and belong to class

    _____.

6. Fast, creepy predatory arthropods having one pair of legs per segment are the

    _____ and belong to class

    _____

7. List five general characteristics of a large group of arthropods called the
    crustaceans.

    a. _____

    b. _____

    c. _____

    d. _____

    e. _____

8.   Sessile or stalked crustaceans called _____

are covered in calcareous plates and use their wispy legs (cirri) to filter-feed

on plankton.

9.   A group of crustaceans, many of which are popular among seafood lovers,

that have ten walking legs, are the _____.

10.   Label the crayfish with these body parts: carapace, cephalothorax, feeding

appendages, walking legs (specify the chelipeds), abdomen, telson, uropods,

swimmerets, antennules, antennae, and compound eye.

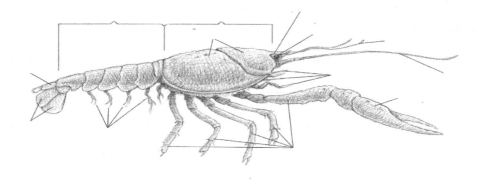

11.   A group of crustaceans that is dorso-ventrally flattened and has seven pairs

of legs is called the _____. List two

extremely different habitats that these crustaceans can be found in.

a.   _____

b.   _____

12.   A group of crustaceans that is laterally flattened and also has seven pairs of

legs is called the _____

13.   The largest group of arthropods (by far) possessing head, thorax, abdomen,

_____ legs, _____ wings (if present), and _____

pair of antennae is the insects.

14. Draw and label a generalized insect with these body parts: head, thorax, and abdomen; prothoracic, mesothoracic, and metathoracic legs; forewings and hind wings; antennae, compound eyes, and mouthparts.

15. The forewings of beetles, comprising the biggest order of insects (order _____) are hardened wing covers called _____

16. Order _____ are also known as the flies, have only _____ wings. In place of hind-wings are gyroscopic organs called _____ , which are needed for balance during flight.

17. Order Hemiptera are also known as the true _____ have _____ mouthparts.

18. Butterflies and moths (order _____) have microscopic scales covering their _____ and _____ mouthparts.

19. Beetles, flies, and butterflies, and wasps have _____ metamorphosis because their larval body form is drastically different from their adult body form. The _____ stage is when most of the transformation occurs.

20. True or false? Horseshoe crabs are crustaceans.

21. Arthropods called arachnids have two body regions: the cephalothorax and

    _____.

22. In arachnids, the cephalothorax has _____

    (mouthparts), short sensory leg-like appendages called _____ ,

    and four pairs of _____.

23. Which of the following is not an arachnid?

    a. Ticks

    b. Lice

    c. Mites

    d. Daddy longlegs (harvestmen)

    e. Scorpions

    f. Spiders

24. Spiders may use silk for:

    a. Prey capture.

    b. Prey wrapping.

    c. Making egg sacs.

    d. Lining their nests.

    e. Containing sperm.

    f. All the above.

25. Which of the following are not arthropods?

    a. Insects

    b. Arachnids

    c. Crustaceans

    d. Polychaetes

    e. Centipedes

    f. Millipedes

    g. Horseshoe crabs

PHYLUM ECHINODERMATA
THE ECHINODERMS

OBJECTIVES

1. Know the major characteristics of Echinoderms.

2. Know the distinguishing characteristics and basic natural history of the following classes: Asteroidea, Ophiuroidea, Echinoidea, and Holothuroidea. Also know the common names of the classes.

 Thoroughly study the above objectives before you take the chapter quiz. Be sure you know how to spell the terms.

CHAPTER 26 QUIZ

1. Echinoderm means _____.

2. Name the hydraulic system that all echinoderms share:

    _____

3. Which is not part of this hydraulic system?

    a. sieve plate

    b. stone canal

    c. ring canal

    d. pedicellariae

    e. radial canal

    f. lateral canal

    g. ampullae

    h. tube feet

4. Echinoderm walking appendages are called _____

    and are extensions of the above system.

5. Give the common names of these echinoderm classes.

    a. Asteroidea: _____

    b. Echinoidea: _____

    c. Ophiuroidea: _____

    d. Holothuroidea: _____

6. Which of those classes is known to have the longest spines?

    _____

7. Which of those classes is mostly herbivorous on kelp and other seaweeds and

    uses a jaw-like apparatus called Aristotle's lantern to graze the bottom?

    _____

8. Which of those classes is usually lacking spines and can eviscerate when

    disturbed? _____

9. A predatory sea star can extrude its _____ outside its body and insert it into its bivalve prey.

10. Sea cucumbers collect food on their mucous-coated branching _____. Once enough is collected, it is inserted into its mouth and the food is swallowed.

 Study all the objectives for this unit. Make sure you know the correct answers for the quizzes. Understand the concepts and terms; don't just memorize them. Then take the Unit Exam.

UNIT 9 EXAM

1. List six characteristics of mollusks (one is possessed by most but not all mollusks).

    a. _____

    b. _____

    c. _____

    d. _____

    e. _____

    f. _____

2. The _____ secretes the shell in mollusks.

3. Which class of mollusks are filter feeders? _____

4. The tongue-like rasping organ in many mollusks is the _____.

5. Name three mollusks that don't have a shell of any kind.

    a. _____

    b. _____

    c. _____

6. In bivalves, what organ collects plankton on its surface and sweeps it toward the mouth with cilia? _____

7. In bivalves, what organ is the gateway of water into the mantle cavity?

    _____

8. What organ is the exit of water out of the bivalve? _____

9. By expanding and contracting their mantle, cephalopods accomplish at least two important things. They are:

    a. _____

    b. _____

10. Cephalopods have an _____ from which black fluid is expelled out the funnel to confuse and distract predators in an attempt to get away.

11. Name three types of cephalopods.

    a. _____

    b. _____

    c. _____

12. Name three types of bivalves.

    a. _____

    b. _____

    c. _____

13. Name three types of gastropods.

    a. _____

    b. _____

    c. _____

14. Slugs and land snails have two pair of tentacles. What do the upper ones have at their tips? _____

15. Slugs have a _____ which serves as an organ of respiration.

16. List four major characteristics of the arthropods.

    a. _____

    b. _____

    c. _____

    d. _____

17. Arthropod means _____.

18. In the molting process, the new cuticle is produced _____ the old cuticle.

    a. Underneath
    b. On the outside of

19. An extinct group of arthropods having a head, thorax, and pygidium is the

    _____.

20. Slow, graceful arthropods that feed on lichens, detritus, and some plants and

    have two pairs of legs per segment (on most segments) are the

    _____ and belong to class

    _____.

21. Fast, creepy predatory arthropods having one pair of legs per segment are the

    _____ and belong to class

    _____.

22. List five general characteristics of a large group of arthropods called the
    crustaceans.

    a. _____

    b. _____

    c. _____

    d. _____

    e. _____

23. Sessile or stalked crustaceans called _____

    are covered in calcareous plates and use their wispy legs (cirri) to filter feed

    on plankton.

24. A group of crustaceans, many of which are popular among seafood lovers,

    that have ten walking legs, are the _____.

25. Label the crayfish with these body parts: carapace, cephalothorax, feeding appendages, walking legs (specify the chelipeds), abdomen, telson, uropods, swimmerets, antennules, antennae, and compound eye.

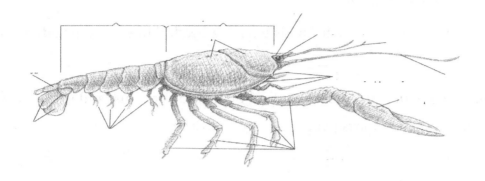

26. A group of crustaceans that is dorso-ventrally flattened and has seven pairs of legs is called the _____. List two extremely different habitats that these crustaceans can be found in.

    a. _____

    b. _____

27. A group of crustaceans that is laterally flattened and also has seven pairs of legs is called the _____

28. The largest group of arthropods (by far) possessing head, thorax, abdomen, _____ legs, _____ wings (if present), and _____ pair of antennae is the insects.

29. Draw and label a generalized insect with these body parts: head, thorax, and abdomen; prothoracic, mesothoracic, and metathoracic legs; forewings and hind wings; antennae, compound eyes, and mouthparts.

30. The forewings of beetles are hardened wing covers called _____ . Beetles comprise the biggest order of insects, called _____ .

31. Order _____, also known as the flies, have only _____ wings. In place of hind-wings are gyroscopic organs called _____ needed for balance during flight.

32. Order Hemiptera are also known as the true _____ have _____ mouthparts.

33. Butterflies and moths (order _____) have microscopic scales covering their _____ and _____ mouthparts.

34. Beetles, flies, and butterflies, and wasps have _____ metamorphosis because their larval body form is drastically different from their adult body form. The _____ stage is when most of the transformation occurs.

35. True or false? Horseshoe crabs are crustaceans.

36. Arthropods called arachnids have two body regions: the cephalothorax and

    _____.

37. In arachnids, the cephalothorax has _____

    (mouthparts), short sensory leg-like appendages called _____

    and four pairs of _____.

38. Which of the following is not an arachnid?

    a. Ticks

    b. Lice

    c. Mites

    d. Daddy longlegs (harvestmen)

    e. Scorpions

    f. Spiders

39. Spiders may use silk for:

    a. Prey capture.

    b. Prey wrapping.

    c. Making egg sacs.

    d. Lining their nests.

    e. Containing sperm.

    f. All the above.

40. Which of the following are not arthropods?

    a. Insects

    b. Arachnids

    c. Crustaceans

    d. Polychaetes

    e. Centipedes

    f. Millipedes

    g. Horseshoe crabs

41. Echinoderm means _____.

42. Name the hydraulic system that all echinoderms share.

_____

43. Which is not part of this hydraulic system?

    a. sieve plate

    b. stone canal

    c. ring canal

    d. pedicellariae

    e. radial canal

    f. lateral canal

    g. ampullae

    h. tube feet

44. Echinoderm walking appendages are called _____ and are extensions of the above system.

45. Give the common names of these echinoderm classes.

    a. Asteroidea: _____

    b. Echinoidea: _____

    c. Ophiuroidea: _____

    d. Holothuroidea: _____

46. Which class is known to have the longest spines? _____

47. Which class is mostly herbivorous on kelp and other seaweeds and uses a jaw-like apparatus called Aristotle's lantern to graze the bottom?

_____

48. Which class is usually lacking spines and can eviscerate when disturbed? ____

_____

49. A predatory sea star can extrude its _____ outside its body and insert it into its bivalve prey.

50. Sea cucumbers collect food on their mucous-coated branching
_____. Once enough is collected, it
is inserted into its mouth and the food is swallowed.

PHYLUM CHORDATA

THE CHORDATES

OBJECTIVES

1. Know the major characteristics of Chordates.

2. Know the distinguishing characteristics and basic natural history of the three subphyla of Chordates.

3. Know the major characteristics, representative examples, and basic natural history of the following taxa of vertebrates (mostly classes and selected orders): Agnatha, Chondrichthyes, Osteichthyes, Amphibia, Reptilia, Aves, and Mammalia. In the case of amphibian and reptilian orders, know the major characteristics, representative examples, and their basic natural history. In the case of the selected bird and mammal orders, be able to recognize representative examples and know what order they belong in.

 Thoroughly study the above objectives before you take the chapter quiz. Be sure you know how to spell the terms.

CHAPTER 27 QUIZ

1. Sea squirts belong to _____.

    a. Urochordata

    b. Cephalochordata

    c. Vertebrata

2. Lancelets belong to _____.

    a. Urochordata

    b. Cephalochordata

    c. Vertebrata

3. What is unique about the mouth of lampreys and hagfish (the agnathans)?

    _____

4. What is unique about the skeleton (except the jaw) of all sharks, skates, rays chimaeras, and sawfish? _____

5. Sharks, skates, rays, etc. belong to the class _____.

6. Class Osteichthyes are the _____ fish and include (list three examples that highlight some of the extreme differences in this group).

    a. _____

    b. _____

    c. _____

7. The gill covering called the operculum is a feature of _____.

    a. Bony fish

    b. Hagfish

    c. Lampreys

    d. Chondrichthyes

8.   What type of fertilization do most frogs and toads (order Anura) exhibit?

    a. internal

    b. external

9.   What is the order or common name of a legless group of tropical amphibians?

    _____

10. Which amphibian order employs a spermatophore to inseminate the female resulting in internal fertilization? _____

11. What is the common name for order Testudines? _____

12. Most amphibians can breathe using both lungs and _____ .

13. True or false? All frogs are oviparous (lay eggs).

14. List two main groups of order Squamata.

    a. _____

    b. _____

15. Name one feature that is unique to order Squamata (other reptiles don't have it).

    _____

16. Name one feature that is unique to order Testudines (other reptiles don't have it).

    _____

17. Name two general characteristics of *all birds* that would be considered synapomorphies by evolutionists, in that the presumed reptilian ancestor didn't have them?

    a. _____

    b. _____

18. Match the following to the correct order.

Duck _____   a. Order Passeriformes

Sparrow _____   b. Order Falconiformes

Penguin _____   c. Order Galliformes

Ostrich _____   d. Order Sphenisciformes

Turkey _____   e. Order Struthioniformes

Hawk _____   f. Order Anseriformes

19. What two chordate (vertebrate) classes are endothermic?

   a. _____

   b. _____

20. Name two general characteristics of *all mammals* that would be considered synapomorphies by evolutionists, in that the presumed reptilian ancestor didn't have them.

   a. _____

   b. _____

21. Name two general characteristics of *all reptiles* that would be considered synapomorphies by evolutionists, in that the presumed amphibian ancestor didn't have them.

   a. _____

   b. _____

22. Match the following to the correct order.

   Fruit bat _____   a. Order Rodentia

   Sperm whale _____   b. Order Marsupalia

   Beaver _____   c. Order Chiroptera

   Horse _____   d. Order Artiodactyla

Cougar _____   e. Order Perissodactyla

Deer _____   f. Order Cetacea

Kangaroo _____   g. Order Carnivora

23. Which of the following are not vertebrates?

    a. lampreys and hagfish

    b. cuttlefish

    c. cartilage fish

    d. bony fish

    e. amphibians

    f. reptiles

    g. birds

    h. mammals

KINGDOM PLANTAE

PLANTS

OBJECTIVES

1. Know the major characteristics of Kingdom Plantae.

2. Be able to explain the alteration of generations.

3. Be able to explain the basic life cycles of the following four phyla of plants: mosses, ferns, conifers, and flowering plants. Know the anatomy of each group but especially anatomy which is relevant to their reproduction. Know how they all conform to the alteration of generations.

4. Be able to draw a simple sketch of the different types of leaf morphologies and leaf arrangements.

5. Know the major distinctions between eudicots and monocots.

6. Be able to draw a longitudinal section of a complete flower and label all the floral parts. Be able to trace the path of a pollen tube.

 Thoroughly study the above objectives before you take the chapter quiz. Be sure you know how to spell the terms.

CHAPTER 28 QUIZ

1. Which of the following is *not* a characteristic of Plantae?

    a. autotrophic

    b. multicellular

    c. chitin cell walls

    d. cell plate formation in cytokinesis

    e. contains chloroplasts

2. In the alternation of generations life cycle, sporophytes produce

    _____ within a structure called a sporangium,

    through a cellular division called _____.

3. What is the ploidy of the gametophyte generation?

    a. Diploid

    b. Haploid

4. In mosses, what is the generation composed of a slender leafless stalk with a

    knob on top? _____

5. Answer the following questions about ferns:

    a. What are the visible spots on the undersides of fern pinnae called?

    _____

    b. What is each spot on fern pinnae composed of? _____

    c. What structure in fern sporangia fling the spores abroad in a catapult fashion?

    _____

6. Which phylum of plants has a more conspicuous or dominant gametophyte

    generation?

    a. Flowering plants

    b. Conifers

    c. Ferns

    d. Mosses

7.   Pine, spruce, fir, and cedar belong in the phylum _____.

8.   Male cones of conifers are made up of many tiny microsporangia which release

microgametophytes which are also known as _____.

9.   Female cones of conifers have many woody _____

scales each of which bears two ovules on its upper surface.

10.   In conifers, successful pollination is achieved when pollen grain(s) of the

correct species lands near the _____

(opening in the integument) of the ovule within a female cone.

11.   List four main differences between the two main classes of flowering plants,

the dicots and the monocots.

Dicots   Monocots

_____   _____

_____   _____

_____   _____

_____   _____

12.   In flowering plants pollination is simply the transfer of pollen to a receptive

_____. Name two very different creatures

(from different phyla) that can serve as pollinators.

a.   _____

b.   _____

13.   In flowering plants sperm comes from within the _____ .

14.   In flowering plants the egg is within the ovule which is within the

_____.

15. Draw a simple longitudinal section of a complete flower. With a clear, neat line trace the growth of the pollen tube. Also label the pistil composed of stigma, style, ovary and ovule, and stamen composed of filament and anther.

THE BASICS *of* ECOLOGY

OBJECTIVES

1. Know and understand the definition of ecology. Be able to describe how ecology slightly differs from natural history.

2. Be able to define the following ecological terms: population, community, ecosystem, biotic factors, abiotic factors, habitat, microhabitat, and ecological niche.

3. Be able to describe the following community interactions and be able to give examples of each along with their corresponding symbols.
   - Predator-prey relationships
   - Symbiosis—mutualism, commensalism, and parasitism (ecto and endoparasites)
   - Competition—interspecific and intraspecific competition

4. Know how a population's intrinsic rate of increase is calculated.

5. Be able to graphically represent the following types of population growth: exponential growth and logistic growth. Understand the significance of carrying capacity and the factors that can cause it to vary over time.

6. Be able to interpret the following diagrams of energy flow in ecosystems: food chains, food webs, trophic pyramids. Understand where producers, primary consumers, secondary consumers, tertiary consumers, and decomposers fit into these diagrams.

7. Be able to describe the following biogeochemical cycles: water cycle, carbon cycle, and nitrogen cycle.

8. Be able to give a biblical basis for biodiversity conservation using scriptural references.

 Thoroughly study the above objectives before you take the chapter quiz. Be sure you know how to spell the terms.

CHAPTER 29 QUIZ

1. The study of the interactions between living creatures and their environment is called _____.

2. A naturally functioning system comprised of a living (biotic) community and its nonliving (abiotic) environment is a(n) _____

3. Name the three types of symbioses and their corresponding symbols.

    a. _____

    b. _____

    c. _____

4. Give one example of a pair of creatures in a mutualistic relationship

    _____

5. Give one example of a pair of creatures in a ectoparasitic relationship

    _____

6. In logistic growth what prevents a population from continuing to grow exponentially? _____

7. Which diagram more accurately represents the complex and variable energy flow in a community?

    a. Food web
    b. Food chain
    c. Trophic pyramid

8. Which diagram shows the relative abundance of producers, primary consumers, secondary consumers, etc.?

    a. Food web

    b. Food chain

    c. Trophic pyramid

9.   What two major groups are decomposers?

     a.   _____

     b.   _____

10.   Animals (or plants) within the same population often compete for food, water, territory, sunlight, or mates. This is called _____ competition.

11.   The total lifestyle of an organism including its habitat requirements (both biotic and abiotic) and how it uses these requirements to survive and reproduce are all part of its ecological _____.

12.   When animals, plants, fungi, bacteria, and protists burn glucose during cellular respiration and release (or exhale) CO_2, it is a very important part of what biogeochemical cycle? _____

13.   Name one other plant process that is also part of this cycle:

     _____

14.   Ammonification, nitrogen fixation, nitrification, denitrification are all parts of the _____ cycle.

15.   When atmospheric nitrogen is converted into ammonia by bacteria it is called

     _____.

   Study all the objectives for this unit. Make sure you know the correct answers for the quizzes. Understand the concepts and terms; don't just memorize them. Then take the Unit Exam.

UNIT 10 EXAM

1. Sea squirts belong to _____.
    a. Urochordata
    b. Cephalochordata
    c. Vertebrata

2. Lancelets belong to _____.
    a. Urochordata
    b. Cephalochordata
    c. Vertebrata

3. What is unique about the mouth of lampreys and hagfish (the agnathans)?

    _____

4. What is unique about the skeleton (except the jaw) of all sharks, skates, rays chimaeras, and sawfish? _____

5. Sharks, skates, rays, etc. belong to the class _____.

6. Class Osteichthyes are the _____fish and include (list three examples that highlight some of the extreme differences in this group).

    a. _____
    b. _____
    c. _____

7. The gill covering called the operculum is a feature of _____.
    a. Bony fish
    b. Hagfish
    c. Lampreys
    d. Chondrichthyes

8. What type of fertilization do most frogs and toads (order Anura) exhibit? _____
    a. internal
    b. external

9.   Which amphibian order employs a spermatophore to inseminate the female resulting in internal fertilization? _____

10. What is the common name for order Testudines? _____

11. Most amphibians can breathe using both lungs and _____ .

12. List two main groups of order Squamata.

     a. _____

     b. _____

13. Name one feature that is unique to order Squamata (other reptiles don't have it).

     _____

14. Name one feature that is unique to order Testudines (other reptiles don't have it).

     _____

15. Name two general characteristics of *all birds* that would be considered synapomorphies by evolutionists, in that the presumed reptilian ancestor didn't have them?

     a. _____

     b. _____

16. Match the following to the correct order.

     Duck _____   a. Order Passeriformes

     Sparrow _____   b. Order Falconiformes

     Penguin _____   c. Order Galliformes

     Ostrich _____   d. Order Sphenisciformes

     Turkey _____   e. Order Struthioniformes

     Hawk _____   f. Order Anseriformes

17. What two chordate (vertebrate) classes are endothermic?

    a. _____

    b. _____

18. Name two general characteristics of *all mammals* that would be considered synapomorphies by evolutionists, in that the presumed reptilian ancestor didn't have them.

    a. _____

    b. _____

19. Name two general characteristics of *all reptiles* that would be considered synapomorphies by evolutionists, in that the presumed amphibian ancestor didn't have them.

    a. _____

    b. _____

20. Match the following to the correct order.

    Fruit bat _____   a. Order Rodentia

    Sperm whale _____   b. Order Marsupalia

    Beaver _____   c. Order Chiroptera

    Horse _____   d. Order Artiodactyla

    Cougar _____   e. Order Perissodactyla

    Deer _____   f. Order Cetacea

    Kangaroo _____   g. Order Carnivora

21. Which of the following are not vertebrates?

    a. lampreys and hagfish

    b. crayfish

    c. cartilage fish

    d. bony fish

    e. amphibians

    f. reptiles

    g. birds

    h. mammals

22. Which of the following is *not* a characteristic of Plantae?

    a. autotrophic

    b. multicellular

    c. chitin cell walls

    d. cell plate formation in cytokinesis

    e. contains chloroplasts

23. In the alternation of generations life cycle, sporophytes produce

    _____ within a structure called a sporangium,

    through a cellular division called _____.

24. What is the ploidy of the gametophyte generation?

    a. Diploid

    b. Haploid

25. In mosses, what is the generation composed of a slender leafless stalk with a

    knob on top? _____

26. Answer the following questions about ferns:

    a. What are the visible spots on the undersides of fern pinnae called?

       _____

    b. What is each spot composed of? _____

    c. What structure in fern sporangia fling the spores abroad in a catapult

       fashion? _____

27. Which phylum of plants has a more conspicuous or dominant gametophyte generation?

    a. Flowering plants
    b. Conifers
    c. Ferns
    d. Mosses

28. Male cones of conifers are made up of many tiny microsporangia, which release microgametophytes which are also known as _____ .

29. In conifers, successful pollination is achieved when pollen grain(s) of the correct species lands near the _____ (opening in the integument) of the ovule.

30. List four main differences between the two main classes of flowering plants, the dicots and the monocots.

    Dicots   Monocots

    _____   _____

    _____   _____

    _____   _____

    _____   _____

31. In flowering plants pollination is simply the transfer of pollen to a receptive _____ . Name two very different creatures (from different phyla) that can serve as pollinators.

    a. _____

    b. _____

32. In flowering plants sperm comes from within the _____ .

33. In flowering plants the egg is within the ovule which is within the

    _____.

34. Draw a simple longitudinal section of a complete flower. With a clear, neat line trace the growth of the pollen tube. Also label the pistil composed of stigma, style, ovary and ovule, and stamen composed of filament and anther.

35. The study of the interactions between living creatures and their environment is called _____.

36. A naturally functioning system comprised of a living (biotic) community and its nonliving (abiotic) environment is a(n) _____ .

37. Name the three types of symbioses and their corresponding symbols.

    a. _____

    b. _____

    c. _____

38. Give one example of a pair of creatures in a mutualistic relationship.

    _____

39. In logistic growth what prevents a population from continuing to grow exponentially? _____

40. Which diagram more accurately represents the complex and variable energy flow in a community?

  a. Food web
  b. Food chain
  c. Trophic pyramid

41. Which diagram shows the relative abundance of producers, primary consumers, secondary consumers, etc.?

  a. Food web
  b. Food chain
  c. Trophic pyramid

42. What two major groups are decomposers?

  a. _____

  b. _____

43. Animals (or plants) within the same population often compete for food, water, territory, sunlight, or mates. This is called _____ competition.

44. The total lifestyle of an organism including its habitat requirements (both biotic and abiotic) and how it uses these requirements to survive and reproduce are all part of its ecological _____.

45. a. When animals, plants, fungi, bacteria, and protists burn glucose during cellular respiration and release (or exhale) CO_2, it is a very important part of what biogeochemical cycle? _____

   b. Name one other plant process that is also part of this cycle.

   _____

46. Ammonification, nitrogen fixation, nitrification, denitrification are all parts of the _____ cycle.

47. When atmospheric nitrogen is converted into ammonia by bacteria it is called

_____.

Study all the objectives for Part 2. Make sure you know the correct answers for all the chapter quizzes and unit exams. Understand the concepts and terms; don't just memorize them. Then take the Comprehensive Exam for Part 2.

COMPREHENSIVE EXAM FOR PART 2

1. What are the seven ranks (taxa) in the classification hierarchy below domain that Linnaeus developed but was added to? Go from general to specific.

    a. Domain

    b. _____

    c. _____

    d. _____

    e. _____

    f. _____

    g. _____

    h. _____

2. Creationists object to evolution when it involves the _____.

    a. Minor modification of a plesiomorphy
    b. Addition of an apomorphy.

3. From an evolutionary perspective, butterfly wings and bat wings would be considered _____ structures because they didn't evolve from the same feature in their common ancestor.

4. The two major groups of prokaryotes are the _____ and the _____.

5. The viral _____ is a protein container for _____ or _____.

6. Most species of bacteria _____.

    a. Are disease-causing (pathogenic).

    b. Do not cause disease but aren't beneficial to the environment.

    c. Perform many beneficial ecological functions.

7. What lives in the tissues of corals that enable them to live in such nutrient poor water? _____

    What do these microscopic tenants produce? _____

    How do they produce it? _____

8. What are the technical names of these seaweed groups?

    a. Brown Algae: _____

    b. Red Algae: _____

    c. Green Algae: _____

9. _____ is a polysaccharide extracted from certain types of red algae and is used as a gel-like material for bacteria to grow on in Petri dishes.

10. Many kinds of brown algae often have an organ called a _____, which is used for anchoring them to the sea floor.

11. Protozoans that get around with and obtain food with cilia are classified in the group called _____.

12. The common feature of all amebas is the _____ which is an extension of the cell used for locomotion and feeding.

13. Many freshwater protozoa have an osmotic problem because they live in a hypotonic environment. What organelle do they possess that helps them cope with the constant influx of water? _____

14. Water molds differ from Fungi in two significant ways.

    a. They have a cell wall made of _____ rather than chitin.

    b. They are _____ (ploidy) for most of their life cycle.

15. List six characteristics of Fungi other than eukaryotic, heterotrophic, and multicellular.

    a. _____

    b. _____

    c. _____

    d. _____

    e. _____

    f. _____

16. The zygomycete fungi reproduce asexually from spores that have been released from knob-like spore containers called _____

17. Ascomycete fungi, during the sexual phase form fruiting bodies called _____. The concave (usually) spore-producing surface called the *hymenium* is formed by one layer of densely packed parallel _____ each containing eight _____.

18. Lichens are formed by a mutualistic relationship between _____ and _____.

19. List five general characteristics of all animals.

    a. _____

    b. _____

    c. _____

    d. _____

    e. _____

20. What is the symmetry where the animal can only be divided into two mirror image halves by only one plane? _____

21. Sponges are _____-feeders because they strain out microscopic plankton from the water that circulates through them.

22. The specialized cells in a sponge that generate the water current, capture, and phagocytose the microscopic plankton are called _____ cells.

23. What important ecological service do sponges perform as they filter feed?

    _____

24. The hallmark characteristic of phylum Cnidaria are the possession of cells called cnidocytes which contain stinging organelles called

    _____ .

25. Once triggered _____ flows into the capsule from the cytoplasm of the cnidocyte, causing the nematocyst to be discharged. Then _____ flows out into the prey through the tube.

26. There are two general body forms of Cnidaria: the _____ and the _____ .

27. Phylum _____ are the flatworms because they are all dorsoventrally flattened.

28. Roundworms...
    a. have tapered ends.
    b. have a complete digestive system.
    c. are round in cross section.
    d. all the above
    e. only a and b
    f. only a and c
    g. only b and c

29. Name three ways earthworms benefit the soil.
    a. _____
    b. _____
    c. _____

30. List six characteristics of mollusks (one is possessed by most but not all mollusks).

    a. _____

    b. _____

    c. _____

    d. _____

    e. _____

    f. _____

31. Which class of mollusks are filter feeders? _____

32. By expanding and contracting their mantle, cephalopods accomplish at least two important things. They are:

    a. _____

    b. _____

33. List four major characteristics of the arthropods.

    a. _____

    b. _____

    c. _____

    d. _____

34. Label the crayfish with these body parts: carapace, cephalothorax, feeding appendages, walking legs (specify the chelipeds), abdomen, telson, uropods, swimmerets, antennules, antennae, and compound eye.

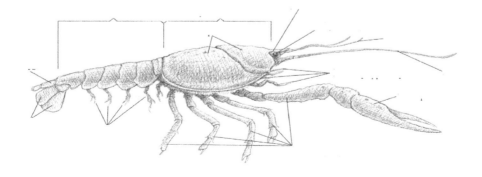

35. Draw and label a generalized insect with these body parts: head, thorax, and abdomen; prothoracic, mesothoracic, and metathoracic legs; forewings and hind wings; antennae, compound eyes, and mouthparts.

36. In arachnids, the cephalothorax has _____ (mouthparts), short sensory leg-like appendages called _____ and four pairs of _____.

37. Which is not part of the water vascular system in Echinoderms?
    a. sieve plate
    b. stone canal
    c. ring canal
    d. pedicellariae
    e. radial canal
    f. lateral canal
    g. ampullae
    h. tube feet

38. Give the common names of these echinoderm classes.

    a. Asteroidea: _____

    b. Echinoidea: _____

    c. Ophiuroidea: _____

    d. Holothuroidea: _____

39. A predatory sea star can extrude its _____ outside its body and insert it into its bivalve prey.

40. What is unique about the skeleton (except the jaw) of fish of Class Chondrichthyes? _____

41. Which amphibian order employs a spermatophore to inseminate the female resulting in internal fertilization? _____

42. What two chordate (vertebrate) classes are endothermic?

    a. _____

    b. _____

43. Name one feature that is unique to order Squamata (other reptiles don't have it).

    _____

44. Which of the following is *not* a characteristic of Plantae?
    a. autotrophic
    b. multicellular
    c. chitin cell walls
    d. cell plate formation in cytokinesis
    e. contains chloroplasts

45. Answer the following questions about ferns:

    a. What are the visible spots on the undersides of the fern pinnae called?

       _____

    b. What is each spot on fern pinnae composed of? _____

    c. What structure in fern sporangia fling the spores abroad in a catapult fashion? _____

46. In conifers, successful pollination is achieved when pollen grain(s) of the correct species lands near the _____ (opening in the integument) of the ovule within a female cone.

47. Draw a simple longitudinal section of a complete flower. With a clear, neat line trace the growth of the pollen tube. Also label the pistil composed of stigma, style, ovary and ovule, and stamen composed of filament and anther.

48. The study of the interactions between living creatures and their environment is called _____.

49. Which diagram shows the relative abundance of producers, primary consumers, secondary consumers, etc.?
    a. Food web
    b. Food chain
    c. Trophic pyramid

50. a. When animals, plants, fungi, bacteria, and protists burn glucose during cellular respiration and release (or exhale) CO_2, it is a very important part of what biogeochemical cycle? _____

    b. Name one other plant process that is also part of this cycle.

    _____

QUIZ AND EXAM

ANSWER KEY

CHAPTER 1 QUIZ

1. element
2. atom
3. compound
4. proton (+), neutron (0)
5. electrons (-)
6. protons
7.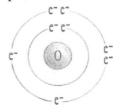

8.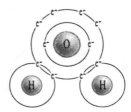

9. ionic
10. covalent
11. polar; non-polar
12. hydrogen
13. hydrogen
14. c. 10 times
15. buffers

CHAPTER 2 QUIZ

1. a. Carbon: 4
   b. Hydrogen: 1
   c. Oxygen: 2
   d. Nitrogen: 3
   e. Phosphorus: 5
   f. Sulfur: 2
2. a. Carbohydrates
   b. Lipids
   c. Proteins
   d. Nucleic Acids
3. Sucrose
4. Polysaccharide
5. plant cell wall material

6.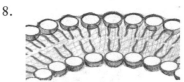

7.

8.

9.

Peptide Bond

10. Protein
11. Polypeptide
12. phosphate

13. 3-D shape; function
14. Any five of the following:
    a. Structural components
    b. Oxygen and CO_2 transport (hemoglobin)
    c. Long-distance chemical messengers
    d. Short-distance chemical messengers
    e. Immunity (antibodies)
    f. Membrane transport (membrane proteins)
    g. Metabolic reactions (enzymes)
    h. Locomotion (flagellar proteins)
    i. Muscle contraction (contractile proteins)
15. a. Rechargeable battery-like molecules
    b. electron shuttle-service

UNIT 1 EXAM

1. element
2. atom
3. compound
4. protons (+), neutrons (0)
5. electrons (-)
6. protons
7. neutrons
8.
9.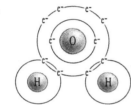
10. ionic
11. covalent
12. polar; non-polar
13. hydrogen
14. hydrogen
15. neutral; acidic; basic (alkaline)
16. c. 10 times
17. buffers
18. a. Carbon: 4
    b. Hydrogen: 1
    c. Oxygen: 2
    d. Nitrogen: 3
    e. Phosphorus: 5
    f. Sulfur: 2
19. a. Carbohydrates
    b. Lipids
    c. Proteins
    d. Nucleic Acids
20. Sucrose
21. Polysaccharide
22. plant cell wall material

23.
    glycosidic linkage
24.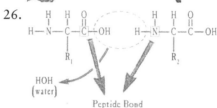
25.
26.

HOH (water)

Peptide Bond

27. Protein
28. Polypeptide
29. phosphate

P   base

sugar

30. 3-D shape; function
31. Any five of the following
    a. Structural components
    b. Oxygen and CO2 transport (hemoglobin)
    c. Long-distance chemical messengers
    d. Short-distance chemical messengers
    e. Immunity (antibodies)
    f. Membrane transport (membrane proteins)
    g. Metabolic reactions (enzymes)
    h. Locomotion (flagellar proteins)
    i. Muscle contraction (contractile proteins)
32. Rechargeable battery-like molecules; electron shuttle-service

CHAPTER 3 QUIZ

1. Telescope
2. Robert Hooke
3. Cellulae
4. The cork cells he observed looked like little rooms in a monastery or prison.
5. Antony van Leeuwenhoek
6. Animalcules
7. 1600s
8. Yes
9. a. All living things are composed of cells
   b. Cells are the basic fundamental unit of all living things
   c. All cells arise from pre-existing cells
10. a. Schwann
    b. Schleiden
    c. Virchow

CHAPTER 4 QUIZ

1. a. Eukaryotic cells have a membrane-bound nucleus
   b. Eukaryotic cells have membrane-bound organelles
   c. Eukaryotic cells are usually larger than 10 micrometers
2. Surface area
3.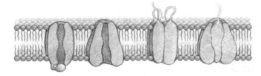
4. The movement of a substance from an area of high concentration to an area of low concentration.
5. Brownian Motion
6. Higher concentration causes a faster diffusion rate.
7. The diffusion of water across a semi-permeable membrane.
8. Lose; plasmolysis; it decreases
9. Active transport
10. endocytosis

CHAPTER 5 QUIZ

1. Nucleus
2. Nucleolus
3. Ribosomes
4. Rough ER
5. Smooth ER; lipids
6. Cytoplasm; water
7. Mitochondrion
8. Chloroplast
9. Golgi body
10. Food vacuole
11. Lysosome
12. Cytoskeletal
13. Microtubules
14. Cell wall
15. Gap

UNIT 2 EXAM

1. Telescope
2. Francesco Stelluti; insects
3. Robert Hooke
4. Cellulae
5. The cork cells he observed looked like little rooms in a monastery or prison.
6. Antony van Leeuwenhoek
7. Animalcules
8. 1600s
9. Yes
10. a. All living things are composed of cells
    b. Cells are the basic fundamental unit of all living things
    c. All cells arise from pre-existing cells
11. a. Schwann
    b. Schleiden
    c. Virchow
12. a. Eukaryotic cells have a membrane-bound nucleus
    b. Eukaryotic cells have membrane-bound organelles
    c. Eukaryotic cells are usually larger than 10 micrometers
13. Surface area

14.

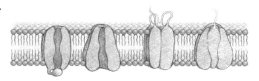

15. The movement of a substance from an area of high concentration to an area of low concentration.
16. Brownian Motion
17. Higher concentration causes a faster diffusion rate.
18. Higher temperature causes a faster diffusion rate.
19. Smaller molecules have a faster diffusion rate.
20. The diffusion of water across a semi-permeable membrane.
21. Lose; plasmolysis; it decreases
22. Active transport
23. Endocytosis
24. Nucleus
25. Nucleolus
26. Ribosomes
27. Rough ER; proteins
28. Smooth ER; lipids
29. Cytoplasm; water
30. Mitochondrion
31. Chloroplast
32. Golgi body
33. Food vacuole
34. Lysosome
35. Cytoskeletal
36. Microtubules
37. Cell wall
38. Gap

CHAPTER 6 QUIZ

1. First Law of Thermodynamics
2. Anabolic reactions build larger molecules from smaller molecules and catabolic reactions break down larger molecules into smaller molecules.
3. Anabolic

4. $C \rightarrow A + B$
5. Enzymes
6. a. Temperature
   b. pH
   c. Concentration
7. Active site
8. Products
9. Metabolism
10. Allosteric

CHAPTER 7 QUIZ

1. $6\ CO_2 + 6\ H_2O \rightarrow C_6H_{12}O_6 + 6\ O_2$
2. Stomates
3. Stomates
4.

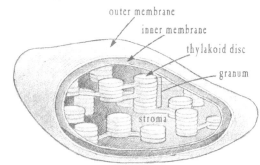

5. Photosystem II; Photosystem I
6. Chlorophyll
7. Antenna
8. Water; NADP+
9. Oxygen
10. Light energy
11. Hydrogen ions
12. Hydrogen; ATP synthase
13. ATP; NADPH
14. Calvin-Benson; Independent
15. Thylakoid; stroma

CHAPTER 8 QUIZ

1. Two
2. Cytoplasm
3. Krebs
4. Pyruvates
5. Two
6. Inner

7.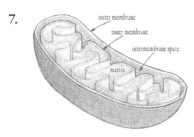

8. NADH; $FADH_2$
9. Three
10. Hydrogen ions
11. Hydrogen: ATP synthase
12. Ten
13. Oxygen
14. It ceases
15. 38

UNIT 3 EXAM

1. First Law of Thermodynamics
2. Anabolic reactions build larger molecules from smaller molecules and catabolic reactions break down larger molecules into smaller molecules.
3. Anabolic
4. C → A + B
5. Enzymes
6. a. Temperature
   b. pH
   c. Concentration
7. Active site
8. Products
9. Metabolism
10. Allosteric
11. $6 CO_2 + 6 H_2O$ → $C_6H_{12}O_6 + 6 O_2$
12. Stomates
13. Stomates
14.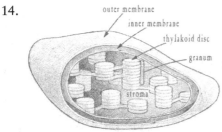

15. Photosystem II; Photosystem I

16. Chlorophyll
17. Antenna
18. Water; NADP+
19. Oxygen
20. Light energy
21. Hydrogen ions
22. Hydrogen; ATP synthase
23. ATP; NADPH
24. Calvin-Benson; Independent
25. Thylakoid; stroma
26. Two
27. Cytoplasm
28. Krebs
29. Pyruvates
30. Two
31. Inner
32.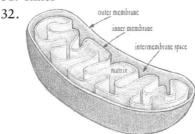

33. NADH; $FADH_2$
34. Three
35. Hydrogen ions
36. Hydrogen; ATP synthase
37. Ten
38. Oxygen
39. It ceases
40. 38

CHAPTER 9 QUIZ

1. James Watson; Francis Crick
2. Maurice Wilkins
3. Rosalind Franklin; Maurice Wilkins
4. a. sugar
   b. phosphate
   c. nitrogenous base
5. a. adenine
   b. guanine
   c. cytosine
   d. thymine

6. Sugar-phosphate
7. Nucleosomes
8. RNA polymerase
9. a. RNA is single-stranded (usually); DNA is double-stranded

   b. RNA has the sugar ribose; DNA has the sugar deoxyribose

   c. RNA has the base uracil; DNA has the base thymine
10. AUG/CGC/GAA/CUA/AAU
11. MET- ARG- GLU- LEU- ASN
12. RNA transcription
13. Transfer RNA or tRNA
14. True
15. Enzymes don't form by chance. You need to have preexisting enzymes to make enzymes.

CHAPTER 10 QUIZ

1. Jacque Monod; Francois Jacob
2. *E. coli*
3. The repressor
4. The promoter
5. Operon
6. Repressor
7. Lactase (beta-galactosidase)
8. Digests lactose into glucose and galactose
9. Permease; it lets more lactose into the cell (permease is a lactose gateway in the membrane)
10. It binds to the operator thus shutting down the operon.

CHAPTER 11 QUIZ

1. Restriction enzymes
2. DNA ligase
3. Sticky ends
4. A cell must be transformed
5. Transduction
6. Bioballistics
7. Conjugation
8. a. Purify DNA containing gene of interest

   b. Cut out gene of interest with appropriate restriction enzyme(s)

   c. Separate gene of interest from DNA it was cut from

   d. Open up purified plasmid with same restriction enzyme

   e. Add gene of interest to opened up plasmid

   f. Splice gene of interest into plasmid using DNA ligase, thus creating recombinant DNA

   g. Transformation of recipient cell with recombinant DNA (plasmid)
9. Insulin
10. Tumor-inducing genes

UNIT 4 EXAM

1. James Watson; Francis Crick
2. Maurice Wilkins
3. Rosalind Franklin; Maurice Wilkins
4. a. sugar

   b. phosphate

   c. nitrogenous base
5. a. adenine

   b. guanine

   c. cytosine

   d. thymine
6. Sugar-phosphate
7. Nucleosomes
8. RNA polymerase
9. a. RNA is single-stranded (usually); DNA is double-stranded

   b. RNA has the sugar ribose; DNA has the sugar deoxyribose

   c. RNA has the base uracil; DNA has the base thymine
10. AUG/CGC/GAA/CUA/AAU
11. MET- ARG- GLU- LEU- ASN
12. RNA transcription
13. Transfer RNA or tRNA
14. Enzymes don't form by chance. You need to have preexisting enzymes to make enzymes.
15. Jacque Monod; Francois Jacob
16. *E. coli*

17. The repressor
18. The promoter
19. Operon
20. Repressor
21. Lactase (beta-galactosidase)
22. Digests lactose into glucose and galactose
23. Permease; it lets more lactose into the cell (permease is a lactose gateway in the membrane)
24. It binds to the operator thus shutting down the operon.
25. Restriction enzymes
26. DNA ligase
27. Sticky ends
28. A cell must be transformed
29. Transduction
30. Bioballistics (Gene gun)
31. Conjugation
32. a. Purify DNA containing gene of interest
    b. Cut out gene of interest with appropriate restriction enzyme(s)
    c. Separate gene of interest from DNA it was cut from
    d. Open up purified plasmid with same restriction enzyme
    e. Add gene of interest to opened up plasmid
    f. Splice gene of interest into plasmid using DNA ligase thus creating recombinant DNA
    g. Transformation of recipient cell with recombinant DNA (plasmid)
33. Insulin

CHAPTER 12 QUIZ

1. DNA replication
2. S
3. DNA polymerase
4. So that both daughter cells get a complete set of genetic information after mitosis.
5. Chromosome
6. Metaphase
7. Prophase
8. Cell plate
9. Anaphase

10. Telophase

CHAPTER 13 QUIZ

1. b. Anaphase I
2. b. Meiosis I
3. b. Anaphase II
4. Homologous chromosomes
5. Prophase I
6. Much more variety in the offspring
7. In metaphase of mitosis, individual chromosomes line up on the plane of division. In metaphase I of meiosis, homologous chromosome line up on the plane of division.
8. Diploid to haploid
9. a. Males: testes
   b. Females: ovaries
10. Gametes—sperm in males; eggs in females

CHAPTER 14 QUIZ

1. Alleles
2. Diploid
3. Haploid
4. Genotype
5. Phenotype
6. Yy x Yy

	Y	y
Y	YY	Yy
y	Yy	yy

7. 75% or ¾
8. Do a test cross
9. YyRr x YyRr

	YR	Yr	yR	yr
YR	YYRR	YYRr	YyRR	YyRr
Yr	YYRr	YYrr	YyRr	Yyrr
yR	YyRR	YyRr	yyRR	yyRr
yr	YyRr	Yyrr	yyRr	yyrr

10. 18.75% or ³⁄₁₆
11. 6.25% or ¹⁄₁₆
12. FfCc x FfCc

	FC	Fc	fC	fc
FC	FFCC	FFCc	FfCC	FfCc
Fc	FFCc	FFcc	FfCc	Ffcc

| fC | FfCC | FfCc | ffCC | ffCc |
| fc | FfCc | Ffcc | ffCc | ffcc |

13. Both parents are fire-breathing and six headed.

14. 12.5% or ²⁄16 or ⅛ of the offspring are not fire-breathing and six headed.

15. 18.75% or ³⁄16 of the offspring are fire-breathing and two headed.

UNIT 5 EXAM

1. DNA replication
2. Answer not written out.
3. DNA polymerase
4. So that both daughter cells get a complete set of genetic information after mitosis.
5. Chromosome
6. Metaphase
7. Prophase
8. Cell plate
9. Cleavage furrowing
10. Anaphase
11. Telophase
12. b. Anaphase I
13. b. Meiosis I
14. b. Anaphase II
15. Plants
16. Meiosis II
17. Homologous chromosomes
18. Prophase I
19. Much more variety in the offspring
20. In metaphase of mitosis, individual chromosomes line up on the plane of division. In metaphase I of meiosis, homologous chromosome line up on the plane of division.
21. Diploid; haploid
22. a. Males: testes
    b. Females: ovaries
23. Sperm
24. Eggs
25. Alleles
26. Diploid

27. Haploid
28. Genotype
29. Phenotype
30. Heterozygous; alleles
31. Dominant; recessive
32. Yy x Yy

	Y	y
Y	YY	Yy
y	Yy	yy

33. 75% or ¾
34. Do a test cross
35. YyRr x YyRr

	YR	Yr	yR	yr
YR	YYRR	YYRr	YyRR	YyRr
Yr	YYRr	YYrr	YyRr	Yyrr
yR	YyRR	YyRr	yyRR	yyRr
yr	YyRr	Yyrr	yyRr	yyrr

36. 18.75% or ³⁄16
37. 6.25% or ¹⁄16
38. FfCc x FfCc

	FC	Fc	fC	fc
FC	FFCC	FFCc	FfCC	FfCc
Fc	FFCc	FFcc	FfCc	Ffcc
fC	FfCC	FfCc	ffCC	ffCc
fc	FfCc	Ffcc	ffCc	ffcc

39. Both parents are fire-breathing and six headed.
40. 12.5% or ²⁄16 or ⅛ of the offspring are not fire-breathing and six headed.
41. 18.75% or ³⁄16 of the offspring are fire-breathing and two headed.

COMPREHENSIVE EXAM FOR PART 1

1. Protons; neutrons
2. Polar; non-polar
3.

4. c. 10
5. Answers may be in any order:
    a. carbohydrates
    b. lipids
    c. proteins
    d. nucleic acids
6. a. Carbon 4
    b. Hydrogen 1
    c. Oxygen 2
    d. Nitrogen 3
    e. Phosphorus 5
    f. Sulfur 2
7.

Peptide Bond

8.

9. Robert Hooke
10. Leeuwenhoek
11. Answers below can be in any order.
    a. All living things are composed of cells
    b. Cells are the basic fundamental unit of all living things
    c. All cells arise from pre-existing cells
12. The movement of a substance from an area of high concentration to an area of low concentration
13. The diffusion of water across a semi-permeable membrane
14. Active transport
15. Ribosomes
16. Chloroplast
17. Lysosome
18. First Law of Thermodynamics
19. Enzymes
20. Active site
21. Stomates
22. Answers below can be in any order.
    a. NADPH
    b. ATP
23. Calvin-Benson Cycle; stroma
24. Cytoplasm
25. Hydrogen; ATP synthase
26. Oxygen
27. 38
28. Answers below can be in any order.
    a. James Watson
    b. Francis Crick
29. Answers below can be in any order.
    a. Adenine
    b. Guanine
    c. Thymine
    d. Cytosine
30. AUG/CGC/GAA/CUA/AAU
31. MET- ARG- GLU- LEU- ASN
32. *E. coli*
33. Promoter
34. Repressor
35. Restriction enzymes
36. DNA ligase
37. a. Purify DNA containing gene of interest
    b. Cut out gene of interest with appropriate restriction enzyme(s)
    c. Separate gene of interest from DNA it was cut from
    d. Open up purified plasmid with same restriction enzyme
    e. Add gene of interest to opened up plasmid
    f. Splice gene of interest into plasmid using DNA ligase thus creating recombinant DNA
    g. Transformation of recipient cell with recombinant DNA (plasmid)
38. DNA replication

39. Metaphase
40. Telophase
41. b. Anaphase I
42. Homologous chromosomes
43. Diploid; haploid
44. b. anaphase II
45. Genotype
46. Phenotype
47. FfCc x FfCc

	FC	Fc	fC	fc
FC	FFCC	FFCc	FfCC	FfCc
Fc	FFCc	FFcc	FfCc	Ffcc
fC	FfCC	FfCc	ffCC	ffCc
fc	FfCc	Ffcc	ffCc	ffcc

48. 12.5% or ²⁄₁₆ or ⅛ of the offspring are not fire-breathing and six headed
49. 18.75% or ³⁄₁₆ of the offspring are fire-breathing and two headed.

CHAPTER 15 QUIZ

1. Aristotle
2. Traits or characters
3. Carolus Linnaeus; binomial
4. b. Kingdom
   c. Phylum
   d. Class
   e. Order
   f. Family
   g. Genus
   h. Species
5. Order
6. Orders
7. *Bufo americanus* or <u>Bufo americanus</u>; Genus—*Bufo*; Species—*Bufo americanus*; Specific epithet—*americanus*
8.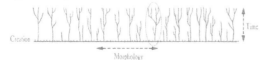
9. Analogous
10. A. monophyletic
11. Homologous
12. Apomorphy
13. Polyphyletic
14. b. Addition of an apomorphy.

CHAPTER 16 QUIZ

1. Capsid; DNA or RNA
2. False
3. False
4. Bacteria; Archaea
5. Peptidoglycan
6. Pili
7. Streptobacillus
8. Plasmids
9. c. Perform many beneficial ecological functions.
10. b. Methanogens

CHAPTER 17 QUIZ

1. Pellicle
2. Stigma
3. Longitudinal; transverse
4. a. Dinoflagellates
5. Diatoms
6. Neurotoxins
7. Zooxanthellae; food; photosynthesis
8. Dinoflagellates
9. Glass or silica
10. Algae
11. Alginate
12. a. Phaeophyta
    b. Rhodophyta
    c. Chlorophyta
13. Pigments
14. a. Holdfast
    b. Stipe
    c. Blade
    d. Pneumatocyst
15. Agar

UNIT 6 EXAM

1. Aristotle
2. Characteristics or traits

3. Carolus Linnaeus; Binomial
4. b. kingdom
   c. phylum
   d. class
   e. order
   f. family
   g. genus
   h. species
5. Order
6. Orders
7. *Bufo americanus* or <u>Bufo americanus</u>;
   Bufo; Bufo americanus; americanus
8.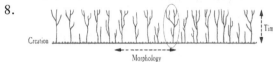
9.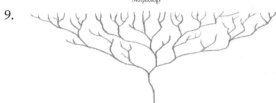

10. Each vertical line represents a species.

11. Charles Darwin
12. Analogous
13. Monophyletic
14. Homologous
15. Apomorphy
16. Polyphyletic
17. b. Addition of an apomorphy.
18. Capsid; DNA or RNA
19. False
20. False
21. Archaea and the Bacteria
22. Peptidoglycan
23. Pili
24. Streptobacilli
25. Diplococci
26. Plasmids
27. c. perform many beneficial ecological
    functions

28. b. Methanogens
29. Salt
30. False
31. Pellicle
32. Stigma or eyespot
33. Longitudinal; transverse
34. a. Dinoflagellates
35. Diatoms
36. Neurotoxins
37. Frustules
38. Zooxanthellae
39. Food (sugars); photosynthesis
40. Dinoflagellates
41. Glass
42. Algae
43. Alginate
44. Brown Algae: Phaeophyta
    Red Algae: Rhodophyta
    Green Algae: Chlorophyta
45. Pigments
46. Brown algae often have four major organs
    that compose their body.
    a. Holdfast
    b. Stipe
    c. Blade
    d. Pneumatocysts
47. Green algae (Chlorophyta)
48. their photosynthetic pigments
49. Agar

CHAPTER 18 QUIZ

1. Flagella
2. Foraminiferans
3. Flagellates
4. Radiolarians
5. Foraminiferans
6. Ciliates
7. Pseudopod
8. Protozoa
9. Contractile vacuole
10. Oral groove
11. Sporangia
12. Amebas

13. a. Cellulose
    b. Diploid
14. Potato blight
15. It caused a great famine in Ireland forcing many to emigrate to the United States.

CHAPTER 19 QUIZ

1. a. Filamentous growth—hyphae
   b. Chitin cell wall
   c. Usually haploid
   d. Extracellular digestion
   e. Unique mitosis and meiosis
   f. Reproduce by spores
2. Extracellular digestion; lysosomes
3. a. Human, animal, and plant disease
   b. Destructive decomposers—food and other man-made products
4. a. Brewing and baking
   b. cheeses with mold growing on them
   c. Antibiotics
   Other options: cyclosporine, composting, mycorrhizae, and food.
5. Sporangia
6. Zygosporangia
7. Rhizoids
8. Conidia
9. Ascomas; Asci; Ascospores
10. Yeast
11. Basidiomycetes
12. Gill; basidiospores
13. Ascomycete fungi; Green or Blue-green algae
14. a. Fruticose
15. Mycorrhizae; sugars; water and mineral

CHAPTER 20 QUIZ

1. a. Eukaryotic cell structure
   b. Lack cell walls
   c. Multicellular
   d. Heterotrophic
   e. Motile
2. Muscle tissue
3. Bilateral symmetry
4. Bilateral symmetry
5. (Answers may vary. May include worms, mollusks, arthropods, and other options.)
6. Radial symmetry
7. a. sea stars (Echinoderms)
   b. sea anemones (Cnidarians)
8. Bath sponge
9. Invertebrates
10. Chordata

UNIT 7 EXAM

1. Flagella
2. Foraminiferans
3. Flagellates
4. Radiolarians
5. Foraminiferans
6. Ciliates
7. Pseudopod
8. Protozoa
9. Contractile vacuole
10. Oral groove
11. Sporangia
12. Amebas
13. a. Cellulose
    b. Diploid
14. Potato blight
15. It caused a great famine in Ireland forcing many to emigrate to the United States.
16. a. Filamentous growth—hyphae
    b. Chitin cell wall
    c. Usually haploid
    d. Extracellular digestion
    e. Unique mitosis and meiosis
    f. Reproduce by spores
17. Extracellular digestion; lysosomes
18. a. Human, animal, and plant disease
    b. Destructive decomposers—food and other man-made products
19. a. Brewing and baking
    b. cheeses with mold growing on them
    c. Antibiotics
    Other options: cyclosporine, composting, mycorrhizae, and food.

20. Sporangia
21. Zygosporangia
22. Rhizoids
23. Conidia
24. Ascomas; Asci; Ascospores
25. Yeast
26. Basidiomycetes
27. Gills; basidiospores
28. Ascomycete fungi; Green or Blue-green algae
29. a. Fruticose
30. Mycorrhizae; sugars; water and mineral
31. a. Eukaryotic cell structure
    b. Lack cell walls
    c. Multicellular
    d. Heterotrophic
    e. Motile
32. Muscle tissue
33. Bilateral symmetry
34. Bilateral symmetry
35. (Answers may vary.)
    a. Worms
    b. Mollusks
    c. Arthropods
    d. Vertebrates
36. Radial symmetry
37. a. sea stars (Echinoderms)
    b. sea anemones (Cnidarians)
38. Bath sponge
39. Invertebrates
40. Chordata

CHAPTER 21 QUIZ

1. Filter
2. Spicules
3. Collar
4. Spongin
5. Radial canals
6. Gemmules

7.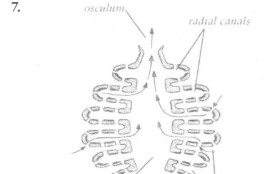

8. Flagellated chambers
9. Keep microscopic plankton levels in check
10. a. The same sponge

CHAPTER 22 QUIZ

1. Nematocysts
2. c. tentacles
3. False
4. Tentacles
5. Water; venom
6. Polyp; medusa
7. Polyp; medusa
8. Gastrovascular; mouth
9. Epidermis; gastrodermis
10. Gastrodermis
11. a. Fish
    b. Sea stars
    Other answers: shrimp, crabs
12. a. Eating
    b. Photosynthesis of zooxanthellae in their tissues
13. a. colony of polyps
14. Mouth; planula
15. Mesoglea

CHAPTER 23 QUIZ

1. Platyhelminthes
2. a. Flukes
    b. Tapeworms
    c. Planarians
3. They live in pre-digested food.

4. a. Flukes
    b. Planarians
5. Fluke
6. Proglottids
7. Scolex
8. Regenerate
9. Pharynx; gastrovascular
10. d. all the above
11. Nematoda
12. They have a complete digestive tract.
13. Lymph; inflammation; elephantiasis
14. Mosquito
15. Annelida
16. a. Class Hirudinea
    b. Class Oligochaeta
    c. Class Polychaeta
17. False
18. a. Aerate
    b. Mix
    c. Enrich with nutrients
19. False
20. Class Polychaeta

UNIT 8 EXAM

1. Filter
2. Spicules
3. Collar
4. Spongin
5. Radial canals
6. Gemmules
7.

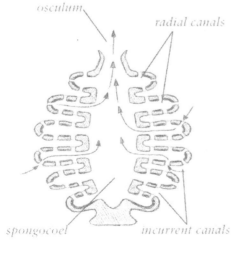

8. Flagellated chambers
9. Keep microscopic plankton levels in check
10. a. The same sponge
11. Nematocysts
12. c. tentacles
13. False
14. Tentacles
15. Water; venom
16. Polyp; medusa
17. Polyp; medusa
18. Gastrovascular; mouth
19. Epidermis; gastrodermis
20. Gastrodermis
21. a. Fish
    b. Sea stars
    Other answers: shrimp, crabs
22. a. Eating
    b. Photosynthesis of zooxanthellae in their tissues
23. a. colony of polyps
24. Mouth; planula
25. Mesoglea
26. Platyhelminthes
27. a. Flukes
    b. Tapeworms
    c. Planarians
28. They live in pre-digested food.
29. a. Flukes
    b. Planarians
30. Fluke
31. Proglottids
32. False
33. Scolex
34. Regenerate
35. Pharynx; gastrovascular
36. d. all the above
37. Nematoda
38. They have a complete digestive tract.
39. Lymph
40. Inflammation
41. Elephantiasis
42. Mosquito
43. Annelida

44. a. Class Hirudinea
    b. Class Oligochaeta
    c. Class Polychaeta
45. False
46. False
47. (in any order)
    a. Fertilize the soil
    b. Aerate the soil
    c. Mix the soil
48. False
49. c. Hirudinea
50. Class Polychaeta

CHAPTER 24 QUIZ

1. a. Mantle
   b. Mantle cavity
   c. Gills or lung
   d. Visceral mass
   e. Head-foot
   f. Shell
2. Mantle
3. Bivalvia
4. Radula
5. a. Slug
   b. Nudibranchs
   c. Octopus
6. Gills
7. Incurrent siphon
8. Excurrent siphon
9. a. Respiration
   b. Locomotion
10. Ink sac
11. a. Octopus
    b. Squid
    c. Nautilus
12. a. Clam
    b. Oyster
    c. Mussel
13. a. Snail
    b. Slug
    c. Conch
14. Eyes
15. Pneumostome

CHAPTER 25 QUIZ

1. a. Exoskeleton
   b. Segmented body
   c. Jointed appendages
   d. Molting
2. Jointed legs
3. a. underneath
4. Trilobites
5. Millipedes; Diplopoda
6. Centipedes; Chilopoda
7. a. two pairs of antennae
   b. a pair of mandibles and two pairs of maxillae
   c. biramous appendages
   d. cuticle with calcium salts
   e. gills for respiration
8. Barnacles
9. Decapods
10.
11. Isopods; a. desert b. ocean floor
12. Amphipods
13. Six; four; one
14.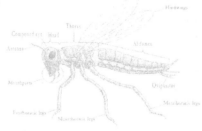
15. Coleoptera; elytra
16. Diptera; two; halteres
17. Bugs; piercing-sucking
18. Lepidoptera; wings; siphoning
19. Complete; pupal
20. False
21. Abdomen
22. Chelicerae; pedipalps; walking legs
23. b. Lice

24. f. All the above.
25. d. Polychaetes

CHAPTER 26 QUIZ

1. Spiny-skinned
2. Water vascular system
3. d. pedicellariae
4. tube feet
5. a. Sea stars
   b. Sea urchins
   c. Brittle stars
   d. Sea cucumbers
6. Echinoidea
7. Echinoidea
8. Holothuroidea
9. Cardiac stomach
10. Tentacles

UNIT 9 EXAM

1. a. Mantle
   b. Mantle cavity
   c. Gills or lung
   d. Visceral mass
   e. Head-foot
   f. Shell (this last item not found in all mollusks)
2. Mantle
3. Bivalvia
4. Radula
5. a. Slug
   b. Nudibranchs
   c. Octopus
6. Gills
7. Incurrent siphon
8. Excurrent siphon
9. a. Respiration
   b. Locomotion
10. Ink sac
11. (Answers may vary.)
    a. Octopus
    b. Squid
    c. Nautilus

12. (Answers may vary.)
    a. Clam
    b. Oyster
    c. Mussel
13. (Answers may vary.)
    a. Snail
    b. Slug
    c. Conch
14. Eyes
15. Pneumostome
16. a. Exoskeleton
    b. Segmented body
    c. Jointed appendages
    d. Molting
17. Jointed legs
18. a. underneath
19. Trilobites
20. Millipedes; Diplopoda
21. Centipedes; Chilopoda
22. a. two pairs of antennae
    b. a pair of mandibles and two pairs of maxillae
    c. biramous appendages
    d. cuticle with calcium salts
    e. gills for respiration
23. Barnacles
24. Decapods
25.
26. Isopods
    a. desert
    b. ocean floor
27. Amphipods
28. Six; four; one
29.

30. Coleoptera; elytra
31. Diptera; two; halteres
32. Bugs; piercing-sucking
33. Lepidoptera; wings; siphoning
34. Complete; pupal
35. False
36. Abdomen
37. Chelicerae; pedipalps; walking legs
38. b. Lice
39. f. All the above.
40. d. Polychaetes
41. Spiny-skinned
42. Water vascular system
43. d. pedicellariae
44. tube feet
45. a. Sea stars
    b. Sea urchins
    c. Brittle stars
    d. Sea cucumbers
46. Echinoidea
47. Echinoidea
48. Holothuroidea
49. Cardiac stomach
50. Tentacles

CHAPTER 27 QUIZ

1.   a.   Urochordata
2.   b.   Cephalochordata
3.   They are jawless.
4.   They are made of cartilage.
5.   Chondrichthyes
6.   Bony
    a. Anglerfish
    b. Seahorse
    c. Eel
7.   a. Bony fish
8.   b. External
9.   Order Gymnophiona or caecilians
10. Order Caudata
11. Turtles
12. Skin
13. False
14. a. Lizards

    b. Snakes
15. Hemipenes
16. Shell
17. a. Feathers
    b. One-way air flow lungs (parabronchi)
18. f. Duck
    a. Sparrow
    d. Penguin
    e. Ostrich
    c. Turkey
    b. Hawk
19. a. Aves
    b. Mammalia
20. a. Hair or fur
    b. Mammary glands
21. a. Scales
    b. Shelled egg
22. c. Fruit bat
    f. Sperm whale
    a. Beaver
    e. Horse
    g. Cougar
    d. Deer
    b. Kangaroo
23. b. Cuttlefish

CHAPTER 28 QUIZ

1.   c. chitin cell walls
2.   spores; meiosis
3.   b. Haploid
4.   Sporophyte
5.   a. Sori
    b. A cluster of sporangia
    c. Annulus
6.   d. mosses
7.   Coniferophyta
8.   Pollen
9.   Ovuliferous
10. Micropyle
11. Dicots:
    Two cotyledons per embryo
    Netted venation in leaves
    Circular arrangement of vascular bundles

in stem viewed in cross section
Floral parts in multiples of 4s or 5s
Monocots:
  One cotyledon per embryo
  Parallel venation in leaves
  Scattered arrangement of vascular
    bundles in stem viewed in cross section
  Floral parts in multiples of 3s

12. Stigma
    a. Insects
    b. Bats
13. Pollen grain
14. Megagametophyte
15. Stamen

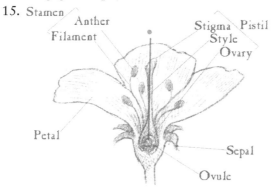

CHAPTER 29 QUIZ

1. Ecology
2. Ecosystem
3. a. Mutualism +/+
    b. Commensalism +/o
    c. Parasitism +/–
4. Lichens, coral and zooxanthellae, sea anemone and clownfish, or ants and the Bullhorn acacia.
5. Leeches and humans, ticks and deer, or fleas and dogs
6. Carrying capacity
7. a. Food web
8. c. Trophic pyramid
9. a. Bacteria
    b. Fungi
10. Intraspecific
11. Niche
12. Carbon cycle

13. Photosynthesis
14. Nitrogen cycle
15. Nitrogen fixation

UNIT 10 EXAM

1. a. Urochordata
2. b. Cephalochordata
3. They are jawless.
4. They are made of cartilage.
5. Chondrichthyes
6. Bony;
    a. Anglerfish
    b. Seahorse
    c. Eel
7. a. Bony fish
8. b. External
9. Order Caudata
10. Turtles
11. Skin
12. a. Lizards
    b. Snakes
13. Hemipenes
14. Shell
15. a. Feathers
    b. One-way air flow lungs (parabronchi)
16. f. Duck
    a. Sparrow
    d. Penguin
    e. Ostrich
    c. Turkey
    b. Hawk
17. a. Aves
    b. Mammalia
18. a. Hair or fur
    b. Mammary glands
19. a. Scales
    b. Shelled egg
20. c. Fruit bat
    f. Sperm whale
    a. Beaver
    e. Horse
    g. Cougar
    d. Deer

b. Kangaroo
21. b. Crayfish
22. c. chitin cell walls
23. spores; meiosis
24. b. Haploid
25. Sporophyte
26. a. Sori
    b. A cluster of sporangia
    c. Annulus
27. d. mosses
28. Pollen
29. Micropyle
30. Dicots:
    Two cotyledons per embryo
    Netted venation in leaves
    Circular arrangement of vascular bundles
      in stem viewed in cross section
    Floral parts in multiples of 4s or 5s
    Monocots:
    One cotyledon per embryo
    Parallel venation in leaves
    Scattered arrangement of vascular
      bundles in stem viewed in cross section
    Floral parts in multiples of 3s
31. Stigma
    a. Insects
    b. Bats
32. Pollen grain
33. Megagametophyte
34.

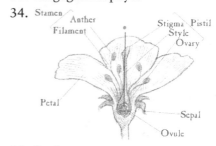

35. Ecology
36. Ecosystem
37. a. Mutualism +/+
    b. Commensalism +/o
    c. Parasitism +/–
38. Lichens, coral and zooxanthellae, sea
    anemone and clownfish, or ants and the
    Bullhorn acacia.

39. Carrying capacity
40. a. Food web
41. c. Trophic pyramid
42. a. bacteria
    b. fungi
43. Intraspecific
44. Niche
45. a. Carbon cycle
    b. Photosynthesis
46. Nitrogen cycle
47. Nitrogen fixation

COMPREHENSIVE EXAM FOR PART 2

1. b. Kingdom
   c. Phylum
   d. Class
   e. Order
   f. Family
   g. Genus
   h. Species
2. b. addition of an apomorphy
3. analogous
4. Eubacteria; Archaea
5. Capsid; DNA; RNA
6. c. Perform many beneficial ecological
   functions.
7. Zooxanthellae; sugars; photosynthesis
8. a. Phaeophyta
   b. Rhodophyta
   c. Chlorophyta
9. Agar
10. Holdfast
11. Ciliophora or Ciliates
12. Pseudopod
13. Contractile vacuole
14. a. Cellulose
    b. Diploid
15. Answers below can be in any order:
    a. Filamentous growth—hyphae
    b. Chitin cell wall
    c. Usually haploid
    d. Extracellular digestion
    e. Unique mitosis and meiosis

f. Reproduce by spores
16. Sporangia
17. Ascomas; asci; ascospores
18. algae; fungi
19. Answers below can be in any order.:
   a. eukaryotic cell structure
   b. Lack cell walls
   c. Multicellular
   d. Heterotrophic
   e. Motile
20. Bilateral
21. Filter
22. Collar cells
23. Keep microscopic plankton levels in check
24. Nematocysts
25. Water; venom
26. Polyp; medusa
27. Platyhelminthes
28. d. all the above
29. Answers below can be in any order:
   a. Fertilize the soil
   b. Aerate the soil
   c. Mix the soil
30. Answers below can be in any order:
   a. Mantle
   b. Mantle cavity
   c. Gills or lung
   d. Visceral mass
   e. Head-foot
   f. Shell
31. Bivalves
32. a. Respiration
   b. Locomotion
33. Answers below can be in any order:
   a. Exoskeleton
   b. Segmented body
   c. Jointed appendages
   d. Molting
34.

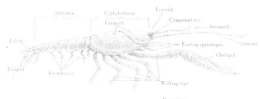

35.

36. Chelicerae; pedipalps; walking legs
37. d. pedicellariae
38. a. Sea stars
   b. Sea urchins
   c. Brittlestars
   d. Sea cucumbers
39. Cardiac stomach
40. It's made of cartilage
41. Caudata or salamanders
42. Aves; Mammalia
43. Hemipenes
44. c. chitin cell walls
45. a. sori
   b. sporangia
   c. annulus
46. micropyle
47.

48. Ecology
49. c. Trophic pyramid
50. a. carbon cycle
   b. photosynthesis

CPSIA information can be obtained
at www.ICGtesting.com
Printed in the USA
LVHW060138081022
730183LV00008BA/173